The Way
of Discipleship

RON STOHLER, Contributing Editor

ISBN: 1500404888
ISBN 13: 9781500404888

Acknowledgments

This book is dedicated to the people of Grace Church and is the tangible expression of our desire to see you live lives that imitate Jesus.

Special thanks to the many authors and contributors who formed The Way of Discipleship. The work began with the pastors and elders of Grace Church. Thanks to those who shared in writing and editing: David Rodriguez, Chris Shore, Tim Ayers, Doug Perrigin, Keith Carlson, Jeff Unruh, Cyndy Parkman, Melody Boyer, Corinne Gunter, Lisa Telford, Brian Daily and Julie Meiners. Thanks to those on our Communications Team for your unique contributions: Katelyn Harbeck, Curtis Honeycutt, Mike Chandler, Kristen Raves and Tyler Bender. Thanks to those who made thorough edits: Mary Lou Stewart and Penny Rodriguez.

Lastly, thanks to the members in the Covenant Community who stepped up to be the first wave of disciplers. Without your input, this resource wouldn't be what it is today. Your work is helping us equip the next generation of Jesus followers.

In Christ,

Ron Stohler
Pastor of Adult Ministries and fellow discipler
Grace Church – 146th St., Noblesville, Indiana

Table of Contents

Introduction

> Therefore go and make disciples of all nations, baptizing them in the name
> of the Father and of the Son and of the Holy Spirit, and teaching them to
> obey everything I have commanded you. And surely I am with you always,
> to the very end of the age.
>
> —Matthew 28:19–20 (NIV)

We're losing the battle. The world is dying faster than we're making disciples.

We live in a culture struggling with emotional exhaustion and disengagement. In pursuit of the mythical American Dream, our society values success and personal comfort over righteousness. Our neighbors grow more isolated, viewing relationships as optional and disposable. Technological distraction and data onslaught impact our memory, stress, even morality. And lastly, the prevailing belief system among young adults is intensely individualized, relative, and based on happiness, peace, security, and feeling good while keeping God at a safe, comfortable distance.[1]

So, how do we respond to Jesus' call to "go and make disciples of all nations?" What's the best way to do this?

In the early days of Grace Church, like many other churches, our main method was Sunday school for children, students and adults. But on one of those Sundays, we announced the sudden elimination of all adult Sunday school classes in favor of home-based small groups for philosophical and practical reasons. Talk about tension.

In time, adult classes eventually crept back into our approach to spiritual growth—they just weren't on Sundays. While we made several attempts at different types of classes and had a consistent commitment to small groups, several research studies revealed a growing trend: a widening gap between *belief* and *practice* among our people. Many professed faith in Christ and belief in certain doctrines, but our lifestyle choices and spiritual behaviors were not consistent with those beliefs. It was apparent classes and groups could only take us but so far. Our people

---

1   Christian Smith, *Soul Searching: The Religious and Spiritual Lives of American Teenagers*. New York: Oxford University Press, 2005.

expressed a need for *someone* to model for them the life of an *ordinary* follower of Christ—not to mention, the world is dying faster than we're making disciples.

But how do we do this now in a mega-church of thousands of people, many who only periodically attend weekend services and aren't connected in small groups or ministry teams?

The answer was found in none other than Christ Himself.

At a landmark pastoral retreat in March 2010, we were convicted to introduce our own relational-based approach to *discipleship*—unheard of in most mega-churches accustomed to staff-led programming. Plus, we had another hurdle to overcome. Several leaders carried baggage related to the term "discipleship." They'd been burnt by misuse of certain well-intentioned discipleship programs. Despite this, we were convinced that discipleship was the best approach and the most accurate term to describe what our people needed. We surveyed both ancient and modern discipleship models to learn what worked and what they had in common. Most models included three key components that helped a person move from being a Christ *believer* to a Christ *follower*: Christ-centered Biblical teaching, Christ-centered practices and intimate relationships. With those components in mind, a final team shaped what we now call The Way of Discipleship.

What's The Way of Discipleship?

The Way of Discipleship is a time-bound, intentional relationship focused on learning and embracing eleven practices essential to following Jesus Christ. The Way of Discipleship leads both the disciple and the discipler to the transformation of *character* and *calling*. Our approach to The Way of Discipleship is based on the practices and teachings of Christ, the history of the church over the last two thousand years, our own church history and reading the signs of the culture we're trying to reach.

A discipleship relationship is the clearest Biblical model offered. It's exactly how Jesus operated. Although He preached publicly to the multitudes and taught in synagogues, the Gospels are filled with examples of His invitation to a few people—*disciples*—to follow Him for a while. He then commissioned those disciples to invite others to follow them as they had followed Him. The Apostle Paul also used this model. He says in 1 Corinthians 11:1 (NIV), "Follow my example, as I follow the example of Christ." A discipleship relationship calls for one person to invest in the life of another. This type of intentional relationship is effective because it impacts both individuals involved. Through the life of the discipler, the disciple has a living example of what it looks like to follow Jesus.

While The Way of Discipleship is simple and clear, it's *not* easy. The ordinary life of a Christ follower is a counter-cultural, revolutionary way to live. While The Way of Discipleship is rooted in communion with God, it isn't a solitary endeavor. It's modeled by a leader and practiced in community. And it's designed to multiply.

What we do at Grace Church is *make disciples of Jesus and launch them into the mission of God.* The way we do this at Grace is through The Way of Discipleship. We will pray more, ask more, challenge more and do more in order to create a culture of Christ followers of character and calling who will change our world in Jesus' name.

Will you help us win the battle? Will you be part of the two-thousand-year-old Kingdom movement Jesus inaugurated on the shores of Galilee? If the answer is yes, then hang on.

It'll cost you your life.

Dave Rodriguez
Sr. Pastor, Grace Church

Getting Started

Before You Begin

Unlike a book you would read on your own, this book is designed to be used by a discipler who has invited another into a discipleship relationship. Both the discipler and disciple need a copy of this guide to facilitate discussion and personal application. The discipler should read through the *Discipler Resources* section and take The Way of Discipleship training offered live at Grace Church and at thewayofdiscipleship.org.

Preparation for the First Meeting

Agree to meet for sixty to ninety minutes at a location that feels comfortable and allows for conversation. Use the questions below to begin getting to know one another. If you already have a strong relationship, either skip directly to Meeting Two or build on what you already know.

While you're together, discuss the following:

1. When did you first make the decision to follow Christ? What brought you to that point in your life?
2. What did you understand of God, Jesus, and the Holy Spirit when you first believed?
3. How might you describe yourself at the time you made the decision to follow Christ?
4. Describe your upbringing. How has it impacted you and your relationship with Christ?
5. Have you ever been involved in a discipleship or mentoring relationship before? What did it look like? How did it impact you?

 Introduce the Big Idea for The Way of Discipleship

The Way of Discipleship is an intentional, time-bound relationship focused on learning and embracing eleven practices essential to following Jesus Christ.

Key phrases to review:

The Way of Discipleship is the best approach we've found to effectively deepen our relationships with Christ and with others.

An *intentional, time-bound relationship* involves one person inviting another to, for a set period of time, "Follow my example as I follow the example of Christ" (1 Corinthians 11:1). This relationship is designed to obey Christ's mandate in the Great Commission (Matthew 28:16–20). We believe in the multiplication of these relationships, meaning that at some point, a disciple will replicate the relationship with a disciple of his or her own, and so on, and so on.

In order to help new, nominal and mature followers of Christ develop a new way of life based on Jesus' example and core teachings, a disciple must *focus on learning and embracing eleven practices essential to following Jesus Christ.* These practices are defined within this book.

Now, how does this look, practically, for those involved?

Expectations of a "Discipler"

Practically: Each disciple plans his or her meetings differently. Some prefer to schedule them six months to a year in advance, while others plan for only a few meetings at a time. Whatever method you choose, make sure the time is directed toward the goal of the relationship: to explore together the eleven practices essential to following Christ.

Spiritually: It's extremely important for the discipler to prepare for each meeting. Because he or she is taking on the responsibility of spiritually nurturing another soul, a discipler needs to spend time both examining the Scriptures and praying for his or her disciple. Disciplers need to be transparent and communicate to their disciples how each practice is lived out in their own lives.

Expectations of a "Disciple"

Practically: Disciples need to make sure they're faithful to attend meetings and complete any follow-up work assigned during those meetings. This is an *intentional relationship*; the discipler is giving his or her time and efforts to deepen the life and practices of the disciple, so time together should be a priority for both individuals.

Spiritually: Those being discipled should pray for their disciplers. Disciples will invest time into the reading the Bible and into studying The Way of Discipleship practices. A reminder for those being discipled: change takes time; avoid rushing and being tempted to believe there are "quick fixes" for patterns that have taken years to root and surface.

Time Investment

There are typically three sessions dedicated to each of the eleven practices. The guides in this book (along with introduction and conclusion sessions) total about forty sessions. *We recommend meeting every two to three weeks, which is roughly a two-year commitment.* A planning calendar is provided in the back of this book to help you plan time together.
- 40 sessions, 1 every 1 week = 40 weeks, about 9 months, less than 1 year
- 40 sessions, 1 every 2 weeks = 80 weeks, about 18 months, about 1.5 years
- 40 sessions, 1 every 3 weeks = 120 weeks, about 27 months, about 2.25 years
- 40 sessions, 1 every 4 weeks = 160 weeks, about 38 months, about 3 years

Is this worth your time?

The effectiveness of this relationship will be determined by the willingness of both the discipler and disciple to be prepared, commit to learning the practices, and resolve to stay on schedule.

Discussion Prompts and Questions:

1. How is this relationship different than just mentoring or a spiritual friendship?
2. What are some of your hopes and expectations?
3. What are some of your fears or anxieties?

Close in prayer and plan on the next meeting date and material to cover. In preparation for the next meeting, read through the appropriate section and complete the questions, exercises and Scripture readings.

Preparation for the Second Meeting

Before launching into the process of learning and embracing the practices of a disciple of Jesus, we must consider what constitutes actually being a disciple of Jesus.

1. What kind of person did Jesus have in mind when He sought out disciples?
2. What's the difference between being a Christian and being a disciple or Christ follower?
3. What separates a disciple of Jesus from everyone else who simply claims the title "Christian"?

Answers to these questions can best be found by looking at the beginnings of the discipler/ disciple relationship in the story of Jesus and His first disciples:

Matthew 4:18–22 (NIV) *Jesus was walking beside the Sea of Galilee, he saw two brothers, Simon called Peter and his brother Andrew. They were casting a net into the lake, for they were fishermen. "Come, follow me," Jesus said, "and I will send you out to fish for people." At once they left their nets and followed him.*

Going on from there, he saw two other brothers, James son of Zebedee and his brother John. They were in a boat with their father Zebedee, preparing their nets. Jesus

Notes:

called them, and immediately they left the boat and their father and followed him.

Matthew 7:13–14 (NIV) *Enter through the narrow gate. For wide is the gate and broad is the road that leads to destruction, and many enter through it. But small is the gate and narrow the road that leads to life, and only a few find it.*

Matthew 5:1–16 (NIV) *Now when Jesus saw the crowds, he went up on a mountainside and sat down. His disciples came to him, and he began to teach them. He said:*

"Blessed are the poor in spirit,
for theirs is the kingdom of heaven.
Blessed are those who mourn,
for they will be comforted.
Blessed are the meek,
for they will inherit the earth.
Blessed are those who hunger and thirst for righteousness,
for they will be filled.
Blessed are the merciful,
for they will be shown mercy.
Blessed are the pure in heart,
for they will see God.
Blessed are the peacemakers,
for they will be called children of God.
Blessed are those who are persecuted because of righteousness,
for theirs is the kingdom of heaven.
Blessed are you when people insult you, persecute you and falsely say all kinds of evil against you because of me. Rejoice and be glad, because great is your reward in heaven,

Notes:

for in the same way they persecuted the prophets who were before you.
You are the salt of the earth. But if the salt loses its saltiness, how can it be made salty again? It is no longer good for anything, except to be thrown out and trampled underfoot.

You are the light of the world. A town built on a hill cannot be hidden. Neither do people light a lamp and put it under a bowl. Instead they put it on its stand, and it gives light to everyone in the house. In the same way, let your light shine before others, that they may see your good deeds and glorify your Father in heaven."

Matthew 7:24–29 (NIV) *"Therefore everyone who hears these words of mine and puts them into practice is like a wise man who built his house on the rock. The rain came down, the streams rose, and the winds blew and beat against that house; yet it did not fall, because it had its foundation on the rock. But everyone who hears these words of mine and does not put them into practice is like a foolish man who built his house on sand. The rain came down, the streams rose, and the winds blew and beat against that house, and it fell with a great crash." When Jesus had finished saying these things, the crowds were amazed at his teaching, because he taught as one who had authority, and not as their teachers of the law.*

Mark 8:34 (NLT) *Then, calling the crowd to join his disciples, he said, "If any of you wants to be my follower, you must turn from your selfish ways, take up your cross, and follow me."*

Notes:

Luke 9:57–62 (NIV) *As they were walking along the road, a man said to him, "I will follow you wherever you go." Jesus replied, "Foxes have dens and birds have nests, but the Son of Man has no place to lay his head." He said to another man, "Follow me." But he replied, "Lord, first let me go and bury my father." Jesus said to him, "Let the dead bury their own dead, but you go and proclaim the kingdom of God." Still another said, "I will follow you, Lord; but first let me go back and say goodbye to my family." Jesus replied, "No one who puts a hand to the plow and looks back is fit for service in the kingdom of God."*

Luke 10:38–42 (NIV) *As Jesus and his disciples were on their way, he came to a village where a woman named Martha opened her home to him. She had a sister called Mary, who sat at the Lord's feet listening to what he said. But Martha was distracted by all the preparations that had to be made. She came to him and asked, "Lord, don't you care that my sister has left me to do the work by myself? Tell her to help me!" "Martha, Martha," the Lord answered, "you are worried and upset about many things, but few things are needed—or indeed only one. Mary has chosen what is better, and it will not be taken away from her."*

John 6:60–66 (NIV) *On hearing it, many of his disciples said, "This is a hard teaching. Who can accept it?" Aware that his disciples were grumbling about this, Jesus said to them, "Does this offend you? Then what if you see the Son of Man ascend to where he was before! The Spirit gives life; the flesh counts for nothing. The words I have spoken to you—they are full of the Spirit and life. Yet there are some of you who do not believe." For Jesus had known from the beginning which of them did not believe and who would betray him. He went on to say, "This is why I told you that no one can come to me unless the Father has enabled them."*

Notes:

From this time many of his disciples turned back and no
longer followed him.

For both discipler and potential disciple, examine your readiness by honestly answering the following questions before your next meeting and discussing them when you meet again.

Discipler

1. Am I committed to this relationship, humbly taking the lead by example and intentionality?
2. Am I committed to learning more about the Eleven Practices of an Ordinary Disciple?
3. Do I have a heart to invest into my disciple?
4. Do I understand that I'm
   - not perfect?
   - not a Bible scholar or teacher?
   - committed to personal growth?
   - trying to be humble and self-aware?
   - growing in moral consistency and strength of character?

Disciple

1. Am I committed to this intentional relationship, humbly following the lead of my discipler?
2. Am I committed to growing as a follower of Jesus?
3. Am I willing to be
   - teachable?
   - available?
   - open to the work of the Holy Spirit?
   - on the other side of the discipleship relationship in time?
4. Am I currently free of
   - a significant relational conflict?
   - unaddressed pattern(s) of addiction?
   - limiting life circumstance(s)?

Discussion Prompts and Questions:

Whom am I?
Why am I here?

1. Based on the passages you read, how would you define a disciple of Jesus?
2. What might Jesus have had in mind when He was seeking to make disciples?
3. Discuss your readiness. If either of you discerns that you're not ready to move forward, talk about it.

The Philosophy of The Way of Discipleship

Read the philosophy and then discuss the question, "Why are we doing it *this* way?"

The Way of Discipleship leads to the transformation of *character* and *calling*. The Way of Discipleship has two purposes: it shapes the character of the disciple into one of virtue and integrity; and it shapes calling, launching the disciple into the mission of God. The Way of Discipleship won't only change human beings for eternity, it'll also change the world as passionate followers of Jesus who bear fruit in His name.

The Way of Discipleship represents the life of an ordinary follower of Jesus. The Way of Discipleship is a radical call to live as fully devoted followers of Jesus. It's a pathway that leads disciples into a lifestyle based on all of Jesus' teaching (teaching that's best summarized in the Sermon on the Mount). Disciples are required to pattern their lives after Jesus' life in new and concrete ways. However, this is not a pathway that only the most mature or seasoned of Christians dare follow. Rather, it should be the *ordinary* pathway for all followers of Jesus. Jesus' sweeping call to everyone is that they leave everything behind and follow Him. He promises that in following Him, disciples will find that the old lifestyle is gone and everything is now new.

The Way of Discipleship isn't easy. The call to follow Jesus isn't a one-time decision but a lifelong and demanding obedience. Walking in The Way of Discipleship is never easy. It requires choosing daily to die to self as well as a level of faith that absolutely depends on the leading of the Holy Spirit. When disciples begin to walk in this way, they'll understand their desperation and continuing need to be discipled. Because it's so demanding and challenges the status quo in ourselves and others, walking in this new way may lead to suffering, provoke opposition, and possibly incite desertion.

The Way of Discipleship is modeled by a leader and practiced in community. There's no Biblical precedent for a "way of discipleship" that encourages an individual, solitary faith. Jesus requires that His followers live within trustworthy communities and that the relationships in those communities be authentic. Jesus emphasized the importance of relationships by initially inviting His disciples to, "Follow me." You may only live The Way of Discipleship by following another person. Proven, seasoned disciples still offer a similar invitation to others: "Follow me as I follow Jesus." The Way of Discipleship is best *learned* through the modeling of a present fellow disciple and is best *practiced* in the midst of a Christ-honoring community.

The Way of Discipleship is simple and clear. It's a way of life that must be simple enough to undertake and clear enough to understand. This simplicity allows any person (regardless of the depth of his or her relationship with Jesus) to begin to live in this new way. It also has to be clear enough that, once he or she understands it, a person may be forced to decline the invitation to participate as he or she considers the implications it'll have for his or her current life.

The Way of Discipleship is rooted in communion with God. Jesus was in constant communion with God. He lived His life and ministered to others out of a deep relationship with and dependence on His Father. The Way of Discipleship embraces some of the same time-honored practices of Jesus, allowing His followers the space in their lives to be still, resting in the presence of God, which God leads to a deep transformation of character and a clear dedication to actively do that which pleases the Father. Discipleship that is rooted in intimate communion with God results in a radical transformation of the disciple.

Now that you've read through the Philosophy of The Way of Discipleship, can you envision yourself making about a two-year commitment, learning and embracing these eleven practices and eventually leading others in this effort?

Discuss the question, "Why are we doing it *this* way?" Close by reading together the following prayer and planning your next meeting.

Eleven Prayers of an Ordinary Disciple of Jesus

Jesus, I want to live like You today. I want to practice Your ways. I want the world to know that I'm one of Your disciples, living a life that reflects Your character and called to Your purposes in this world. I know I can't do it on my own. So, by Your Holy Spirit, I pray:

1. *Take my life, for I surrender to You again and trust You in everything.*
2. *Come to me, for I long to commune with You, my God.*
3. *Speak to me through Your Word, my daily bread.*
4. *Give me the strength to deny myself for Your sake and the sake of others.*
5. *Guide all my thoughts and actions to reflect Your morality and integrity.*
6. *Remind me that I don't walk this journey alone, but in community.*
7. *Open my ears and heart to seek Your call and the courage to live into it.*
8. *Show me how to demonstrate Your justice and mercy to those I meet.*
9. *Prompt me to generously share the material resources You've given me.*

10. *Help me be inventive in loving others well.*
11. *Use me to lead others to follow You, Jesus.*

In the name of the One I follow, Jesus Christ. Amen.

Preparation for the Third Meeting

Before your third meeting together, review the eleven practices and take the personal assessment that follows.

<u>Psalm 1:3 (NLT)</u> *They are like trees planted along the riverbank, bearing fruit each season. Their leaves never wither, and they prosper in all they do.*

The Eleven Practices of The Way of Discipleship

As roots of a tree below the surface draw on nutrients and the trunk of a tree provides stability, the practices of The Way of Discipleship help shape your **character**. As branches and leaves of a tree spread out, provide shade, bear fruit and multiply, these practices help shape your **calling**.

Practices That Branch Out and Bear Fruit:
- Seeking the Call of God
- Justice and Mercy
- Material Generosity
- Loving Others Well
- Leading Others to Jesus

Practices That Provide Stability:
- Self-Denial
- Moral Integrity
- Spiritual Community

Practices That Deepen Your Roots:
- Surrender and Trust
- Communion with God
- Studying the Word of God

Way of Life

The Eleven Practices of The Way of Discipleship

Practices That Deepen Your Roots

SURRENDER AND TRUST

Ordinary Disciples of Jesus Christ practice surrender to God and trust in Him. Disciples of Jesus Christ surrender their lives to God and live fully, trusting that the Holy Spirit will transform them and give them new lives. They begin their lives of surrender with the admission that, because of sin, all people are separated from God.

Disciples heed God's call to repentance and accept God's offer to forgive their sins and heal their brokenness through faith in Jesus' death and resurrection. They then respond to God's forgiveness by living lives characterized by trust in God, submission to the priorities of God's Kingdom, and the commitment to walk in the Spirit.

COMMUNION WITH GOD

Ordinary disciples of Jesus Christ practice disengagement from their routines and distractions in order to commune with God. As children of God, disciples of Jesus long to be in the presence of their Father. They seek the heart of God and His desires and purposes on a daily basis. They want to know Him, hear from Him and just be with Him. Their desire and need for intimacy with God drives them to alter their lives. They create the time and the environment that allows communion with Him. Disciples of Jesus Christ know that their strength, sustenance, wisdom, and security—their very lives—are rooted in the sacred space of the presence of God.

When disciples of Jesus Christ disengage from their routines and distractions and intimately commune with God, their lives will radically change. Disciples of Jesus who commune with God regularly cultivate sensitivity to the leading of the Holy Spirit, responsiveness to God's Word, security in their identity as children of God, and confidence in exercising their spiritual authority. People around them sense God's presence in them and are drawn into God's presence through them.

STUDYING THE WORD OF GOD

Ordinary disciples of Jesus Christ study the Word of God and take in good Biblical teaching that will transform their lives. Disciples of Jesus are readers and learners. They regularly subject their minds and hearts to the Bible, developing working knowledge of the Scriptures. Followers of Christ believe the Bible speaks to all aspects of life. In addition, ordinary disciples, hungry to know more about God and the Bible, expose themselves to other writings and teaching that help shape their understanding of God, His purposes, their world and themselves.

Ordinary followers of Jesus who study the Word of God and take in good Biblical teaching will experience renewed minds, and their lifestyles will be constantly modified. As they read the Bible and let the Bible impact them, they begin to bear fruit and the dead wood of their lives is trimmed away. The more they read and learn, the more they'll know God. Convinced of its importance, ordinary disciples freely pass on their passion for the Word of God to the next generation.

Practices That Provide Stability

SELF-DENIAL

Ordinary disciples of Jesus Christ practice self-denial. Jesus calls those who follow Him to live in complete and daily abandonment of personal agendas and self-centered desires. He asks disciples to make His Kingdom purposes the priority of their lives. Jesus went so far as to say that those who die to themselves and lose their lives for His sake will not only have their needs provided but will find real life in the process. Jesus intended the Practice of Self-Denial not to be only the lifestyle of a few monastic recluses but to be the normal way for every Christian disciple. It's the way Jesus lived, and it's the way He expects us to live.

When disciples of Jesus Christ willingly live counter culturally by practicing disciplines of self-denial, they experience the fruit of love, joy, peace, patience, kindness, goodness, faithfulness, gentleness and self-control. They're no longer burdened and powerless under their sinful, destructive desires, but they're singularly focused on God's Kingdom and His purposes.

MORAL INTEGRITY

Ordinary disciples of Jesus Christ practice moral integrity. Followers of Christ are urged to live lives worthy of their calling. God has redeemed His children from their formerly empty lives characterized by darkness, ignorance and impurity. Disciples are now empowered by His Spirit and commanded to be holy as God is holy. Ordinary disciples of Jesus are committed to obedience to the commands and principles of God's Word. They're expected to live according to the Spirit rather than their old sinful natures. As God's holy people, there's not to be even a hint of immorality among them. The calling of living as God's chosen people in this world is a high calling and is to be accompanied by a moral life in keeping with that calling.

When Jesus' disciples live moral, holy lives, they honor their Father who's holy and show the world around them an example of a life of integrity. They're credible witnesses to the power of the Gospel. Perhaps the most important result of Christ followers practicing moral integrity is that future generations, their children and grandchildren, will have authentic examples to follow as they also learn to follow Jesus.

SPIRITUAL COMMUNITY

Ordinary disciples of Jesus Christ are committed to living in spiritual communities through local churches. Jesus' disciples hunger for spiritual community—a gathering of fellow disciples; rich, spiritual friendships; and authentic mentoring relationships. They commit to and willingly submit to the authority of that community. Followers of Jesus know the power of authentic, redemptive relationships to encourage and strengthen one another, as well as to draw others to God. They believe "the Bible knows nothing of solitary religion" (John Wesley), and they believe it's a Christ follower's duty to engage others in authentic, redemptive relationships. Christ followers are open and responsive to the rebuke, correction, exhortation, and discipline of the church. Jesus' dream was for His followers to live in unity with one another, and He called them to love one another as He loved them.

Those who commit to these practices know the power of authentic, redemptive relationships. Their lives are shaped and guided by the example and encouragement of others in the faith, and they foster this community in others. When disciples live together in love, unity, and mutual support, their lives and the life of the church of Jesus Christ are strong and powerful in advancing God's Kingdom in this world.

Practices That Branch Out and Bear Fruit

SEEKING THE CALL OF GOD

Ordinary disciples of Jesus Christ seek the call of God on their lives. God created His followers with unique purposes and destinies. Each one has been called to tell God's story and build His Kingdom through that disciple's gifts, abilities and life circumstances. As disciples of Jesus, they must discover and engage their unique calling—whether it means leading people to redemption in Christ, engaging in issues of justice and mercy, providing loving community, or bringing healing and reconciliation. It's up to every disciple of Jesus to move beyond careers, roles, and job titles to discover the callings God has had in mind for him or her since before he or she was even born.

As Jesus' followers live out their callings and mission, with the help of the Holy Spirit, their unique gifts meet the world's unique needs. As a result, they experience a deeper sense of meaning and fulfillment—and the world experiences a deeper change for the good.

JUSTICE AND MERCY

Ordinary disciples of Jesus Christ engage in lifestyles of justice and mercy. Every day we hear of indescribable injustices around the world. Disciples of Jesus aren't only aware of them, but they're also engaged in the mission to confront them. These injustices include the crushing cycle of poverty, the scourge of debilitating illnesses, the constant hatred and hostilities among peoples, the destruction of the physical creation, and the evil of human trafficking, among many others. Ordinary followers of Jesus passionately and actively seek to know their roles in addressing these injustices with selfless hearts motivated by love and service.

When disciples of Jesus engage the world of injustice, things happen. Followers of Christ, through the power of the Holy Spirit, develop compassion and a sense of spiritual authority that courageously confronts the evil systems of injustice. They have the joy of being Jesus in the eyes of the "least of these." As they become more aware of who God is and who they are, they have the thrill of being on "the borderland of the supernatural" where God is actively at work and the enemy is pushing back hard. On occasion, things actually change—people are delivered of spiritual bondage, a child is healed, a woman is rescued, a young man escapes the cycle of poverty, and God's Kingdom agenda is furthered to His glory.

MATERIAL GENEROSITY

Ordinary disciples of Jesus Christ practice material generosity. Ordinary disciples believe generosity should color all of life and determine their financial decisions. They believe deeply that God owns it all. Followers of Christ are wary of the creeping danger of materialism. They desire to leverage as many resources for the church and God's Kingdom as possible and excel at giving. They live their lives under the constant influence of Jesus' teachings on wealth and possessions.

Disciples who practice material generosity are free from the strangling worry of financial bondage. They're also highly productive in God's Kingdom mission, able to engage more freely and frequently in His purposes. Ordinary disciples recognize that the biblical guideline of a tithe (10 percent) is a good starting point for generosity, and they take aggressive steps to give 10 percent or more of their material resources to God's Kingdom purposes. Disciples who practice material generosity experience the joy of God's love as they excel in this practice.

LOVING OTHERS WELL

Ordinary disciples of Jesus Christ love others well. Ordinary disciples of Jesus Christ believe it's their responsibility to love others in the same manner Christ loves them. Their deepest desires are fueled by the passion to love others well. They strive to know others enough to accurately offer the kind of love needed in the moment—compassion, care, forgiveness, and rebuke. Disciples of Jesus practice the Biblical "one anothers," and their lives reflect the interdependence that exemplifies all followers of Jesus.

When disciples of Jesus love in this manner, God uncovers and deals with sin, comforts those in mourning, heals the sick, welcomes the lonely, reconciles those at odds, liberates those under spiritual bondage, and gives guidance to the lost. Disciples who love others well will experience the joy of a life centered on God's high priority of bringing wholeness to others.

LEADING OTHERS TO JESUS

Ordinary disciples of Jesus Christ lead others to follow Jesus. They believe faith in Jesus is the most important aspect of life—so much so that they relentlessly share the Gospel of Christ in both word and deed. They passionately believe God's Spirit can change anyone's life to reflect the life of Jesus, and this conviction leads them to fervently pray for and serve lost and broken people. Ordinary disciples of Jesus see all of life as an opportunity to lead others to Jesus.

Disciples who live with a relentless desire to lead lost people to Jesus experience the joy of engaging with others about new life. They know the wonder of seeing the miracle of Spirit-changed lives. Christ followers have the satisfaction that grows out of participating in this important Kingdom purpose, given to all disciples by Jesus, as those far from God are reconciled to Him and become followers of Jesus.

Personal Assessment

The following assessment will help the discipler and disciple determine the degree to which the eleven practices are currently part of their daily lives. Read through the description of each practice, then complete the assessment prior to your next meeting. Plan to discuss it together the next time you meet.

How frequently do you engage in these practices?

	Almost Never	Rarely	Occasionally	Frequently	Consistently
Ordinary disciples of Jesus Christ practice surrender to God and trust in Him.	☐	☐	☐	☑	☐
Ordinary disciples of Jesus Christ practice disengagement from their routines and distractions in order to commune with God.	☐	☐	☑	☐	☐
Ordinary disciples of Jesus Christ study the Word of God and take in good Biblical teaching that will transform their lives.	☐	☐	☑	☐	☐
Ordinary disciples of Jesus Christ engage in lifestyles of justice and mercy.	☐	☐	☐	☑	☐
Ordinary disciples of Jesus Christ seek the call of God on their lives.	☐	☐	☐	☑	☐
Ordinary disciples of Jesus Christ practice self-denial.	☐	☐	☑	☐	☐
Ordinary disciples of Jesus Christ are committed to living in spiritual communities through the local church.	☐	☐	☑	☐	☐

	Almost Never	Rarely	Occasionally	Frequently	Consistently
Ordinary disciples of Jesus Christ practice moral integrity.	☐	☐	☐	☐	☑
Ordinary disciples of Jesus Christ practice material generosity.	☐	☐	☐	☑	☐
Ordinary disciples of Jesus Christ love others well.	☐	☐	☐	☑	☐
Ordinary disciples of Jesus Christ lead others to follow Jesus.	☐	☑	☐	☐	☐

 While you're together, discuss the following:

Your homework was to take the personal assessment prior to this meeting. Remember, this will help you both figure out to what extent you currently make these eleven practices part of your daily lives.

Discussing the results of the assessment will provide you with a baseline from which to grow as well as give you the chance to consider why you answered the way you did.

Going Forward

Begin with the Practice of Surrender and Trust. Figuring out what it means to fully trust God is foundational to all of the other practices. After completing Surrender and Trust, focus on the other practices that root us in Christ: Communion with God, Self-Denial, Studying the Word, and Moral Integrity. Then, continue to work your way up the tree. Use the schedule at the end of this guidebook. We recommend you meet at least three times for each practice, allowing two or three weeks between each meeting.

Each new section will provide an overview of that particular practice, demonstrating the life of an ordinary disciple of Christ following the practice. Some practices will require more attention and time. Rather than rushing through the practices, the disciple and discipler should use them as outlines for discussion and further study, walking together with God as He works in and through your lives.

For each of the eleven practices, you will notice the following sections:

- Practice Overview
- Preparation For Your Meetings
- Personal Assessment
- Discussion Prompts and Questions
- Scripture

Additional resources including book suggestions, sermons, online tools and other related articles are also available at thewayofdiscipleship.org/resources.

Practices That Deepen Your Roots

The Practice of Surrender and Trust

Salvation: We believe that through faith in Jesus' life, death, and resurrection our sinful disobedience is forgiven and that through repentance and surrender to God we're reconciled to Him for this life and eternity.

—Grace Church Statement of Belief

Preparation for Your First Meeting

Prepare to engage in the Practice of Surrender and Trust by reading each passage below a few times.

Psalm 37:4–7 (NIV) *Take delight in the LORD, and he will give you the desires of your heart. Commit your way to the LORD; trust in him and he will do this: He will make your righteous reward shine like the dawn, your vindication like the noonday sun. Be still before the LORD and wait patiently for him; do not fret when people succeed in their ways, when they carry out their wicked schemes.*

Matthew 16:25: (NIV) *For whoever wants to save their life will lose it, but whoever loses their life for me will find it.*

Matthew 11:28–30 (NIV) *"Come to me, all you who are weary and burdened, and I will give you rest. Take my yoke upon you and learn from me, for I am gentle and humble in heart, and you will find rest for your souls. For my yoke is easy and my burden is light."*

 Practice Overview

Read through the following definition of the Practice of Surrender and Trust. Highlight or underline the words or phrases that stand out to you.

> **Ordinary disciples of Jesus Christ practice surrender to God and trust in Him.**
> Disciples of Jesus Christ surrender their lives to God and live fully, trusting that the Holy Spirit will transform them and give them new lives. They begin their lives of surrender with the admission that, because of sin, all people are separated from God.
>
> Disciples heed God's call to repentance and accept God's offer to forgive their sins and heal their brokenness through faith in Jesus' death and resurrection. They then respond to God's forgiveness by living lives characterized by trust in God, submission to the priorities of God's kingdom, and the commitment to walk in the Spirit.

Record those things that differentiate between your part and God's part in embracing the Practice of Surrender and Trust.

My part: **God's part:**

 Personal Assessment:

	True				Not Sure
I've surrendered my life to Jesus Christ, accepting His forgiveness for my sin.	☐				☐

	Almost Never	Rarely	Occasionally	Frequently	Consistently	Not Sure
I live a life of surrender, in a posture of "palms up" each day.	☐	☐	☐	☐	☐	☐
I live trusting that the Holy Spirit has transformed me and has given me a new life.	☐	☐	☐	☐	☐	☐
I submit my life to the priorities of God's Kingdom.	☐	☐	☐	☐	☐	☐
I live committed to walking in the Spirit.	☐	☐	☐	☐	☐	☐

Discussion Prompts and Questions:

1. If someone were to ask you to describe the Practice of Surrender and Trust, what would you say?
2. How is choosing to surrender and trust both a one-time decision and an ongoing practice? Share any examples of what it's been like for you to practice this in your life.
3. What's currently going on in your life that's requiring you to surrender and trust God in deeper ways?

Interacting with Scripture

Romans 8:1–17 (NLT) *So now there is no condemnation for those who belong to Christ Jesus. And because you belong to him, the power of the life-giving Spirit has freed you from the power of sin that leads to death. The law of Moses was unable to save us because of the weakness of our sinful nature. So God did what the law could not do. He sent his own Son in a body like the bodies we sinners have. And in that body God declared an end to sin's control over us by giving his Son as a sacrifice for our sins. He did this so that the just requirement of the law would be fully satisfied for us, who no longer follow our sinful nature but instead follow the Spirit.*

Those who are dominated by the sinful nature think about sinful things, but those who are controlled by the Holy Spirit think about things that please the Spirit. So letting your sinful nature control your mind leads to death. But letting the Spirit control your mind leads to life and peace. For the sinful nature is always hostile to God. It never did obey God's laws, and it never will. That's why those who

Notes:

are still under the control of their sinful nature can never please God.

But you are not controlled by your sinful nature. You are controlled by the Spirit if you have the Spirit of God living in you. (And remember that those who do not have the Spirit of Christ living in them do not belong to him at all.) And Christ lives within you, so even though your body will die because of sin, the Spirit gives you life because you have been made right with God. The Spirit of God, who raised Jesus from the dead, lives in you. And just as God raised Christ Jesus from the dead, he will give life to your mortal bodies by this same Spirit living within you.

Therefore, dear brothers and sisters, you have no obligation to do what your sinful nature urges you to do. For if you live by its dictates, you will die. But if through the power of the Spirit you put to death the deeds of your sinful nature, you will live. For all who are led by the Spirit of God are children of God.

So you have not received a spirit that makes you fearful slaves. Instead, you received God's Spirit when he adopted you as his own children. Now we call him, "Abba, Father." For his Spirit joins with our spirit to affirm that we are God's children. And since we are his children, we are his heirs. In fact, together with Christ we are heirs of God's glory. But if we are to share his glory, we must also share his suffering.

Galatians 2:19–21 (NIV) *For through the law I died to the law so that I might live for God. I have been crucified with Christ and I no longer live, but Christ lives in me. The life I now live in the body, I live by faith in the Son of God, who loved me and gave himself for me. I do not set aside the grace of God, for if righteousness could be gained through the law, Christ died for nothing!*

Notes:

1. What do these passages tell us about the Practice of Surrender and Trust?
2. How does your life demonstrate trust in God's forgiveness?
3. How is it possible to live "from the Spirit" rather than "from the flesh"?

 Spiritual disciplines are specific actions intended to facilitate spiritual growth and bring about transformation. Integrating spiritual disciplines into your life provides space for you to grow closer to God while yielding to the Holy Spirit's work in making you more like Christ. Over the next few weeks, you'll try some disciplines integral in developing the Practice of Surrender and Trust. Some will be more natural for you, while others may be out of your comfort zone. Over time, you'll find a rhythm that's appropriate to your life stage and spiritual needs.

These are the spiritual disciplines necessary in developing the Practice of Surrender and Trust.

- **Baptism**
- **Communion** (the Lord's Supper, Eucharist)
- **Journaling**
- **Self-examination** (or Examen)
- **Confession**

 Baptism is a public statement and ceremony of commitment and surrender to Christ, symbolizing the death of the old life and the beginning of a new life.

 Baptism

Baptism identifies us with Christ and with the community of believers. The act of baptism with water is a demonstration of our faith in Jesus Christ and representative of his cleansing us of our sins.

Baptism is both an act of obedience and a public declaration of faith in Jesus Christ. Because it's our response to what Christ has done in us, it is, therefore, not a prerequisite to salvation but a symbol of the work that's already taken place.

<u>Romans 6:1–4 (NIV)</u> *What shall we say, then? Shall we go on sinning so that grace may increase? By no means! We are those who have died to sin; how can we live in it any longer? Or don't you know that all of us who were baptized into Christ Jesus were baptized into his death? We were therefore buried with him through baptism into death in order that, just as Christ was raised from the dead through the glory of the Father, we too may live a new life.*

Recount your baptism. What was it like to come to the decision to be baptized? (If you've not been baptized, what's stopping you from taking this step?)

 Communion (the Lord's Supper, Eucharist) is a sacrament or ceremony of remembering the death and resurrection of Jesus through eating and drinking of the symbols of the bread and the cup—the bread representing Christ's body and juice/wine representing Christ's blood, the life-giving atonement for our sins.

When Jesus ate the last supper with His disciples, He broke bread and drank from the cup, telling His disciples to "Do this in remembrance of me."
<u>Luke 22:17–20 (NIV)</u> *After taking the cup, he gave thanks and said, "Take this and divide it among you. For I tell you I will not drink again from the fruit of the vine until the kingdom of God comes."*

And he took bread, gave thanks and broke it, and gave it to them, saying, "This is my body given for you; do this in remembrance of me."

In the same way, after the supper he took the cup, saying, "This cup is the new covenant in my blood, which is poured out for you."

The next time you have the opportunity to participate in communion, make sure to pause and remember. Take time to reflect on the sacrifice Jesus made on your behalf. Take time to confess your sins and shortcomings, remembering you've been forgiven. Each time you participate in communion, remember it's a declaration of both your belief in Jesus and your desire to follow Him.

[To have Faith in Christ] means, of course, trying to do all that He says. There would be no sense in saying you trusted a person if you would not take his advice. Thus if you have really handed yourself over to Him, it must follow that you are trying to obey Him. But trying in a new way, a less worried way. Not doing these things in order to be saved, but because He has begun to save you already. Not hoping to get to Heaven as a reward for your actions, but inevitably wanting to act in a certain way because a first faint gleam of Heaven is already inside you.

—Lewis, *Mere Christianity*

Preparation for Your Second Meeting

 ### Interacting with Scripture

Colossians 3:1–17 (NIV) *Since, then, you have been raised with Christ, set your hearts on things above, where Christ is, seated at the right hand of God. Set your minds on things above, not on earthly things. For you died, and your life is now hidden with Christ in God. When Christ, who is your life, appears, then you also will appear with him in glory. Put to death, therefore, whatever belongs to your earthly nature: sexual immorality, impurity, lust, evil desires and greed, which is idolatry.*

Because of these, the wrath of God is coming. You used to walk in these ways, in the life you once lived. But now you must also rid yourselves of all such things as these: anger, rage, malice, slander, and filthy language from your lips. Do not lie to each other, since you have taken off your old self with its practices and have put on the new self, which is being renewed in knowledge in the image of its Creator. Here there is no Gentile or Jew, circumcised or uncircumcised, barbarian, Scythian, slave or free, but Christ is all, and is in all.

Notes:

Therefore, as God's chosen people, holy and dearly loved, clothe yourselves with compassion, kindness, humility, gentleness and patience. Bear with each other and forgive one another if any of you has a grievance against someone. Forgive as the Lord forgave you. And over all these virtues put on love, which binds them all together in perfect unity.

Let the peace of Christ rule in your hearts, since as members of one body you were called to peace. And be thankful. Let the message of Christ dwell among you richly as you teach and admonish one another with all wisdom through psalms, hymns, and songs from the Spirit, singing to God with gratitude in your hearts. And whatever you do, whether in word or deed, do it all in the name of the Lord Jesus, giving thanks to God the Father through him.

Romans 12:1–2 (NIV) *Therefore, I urge you, brothers and sisters, in view of God's mercy, to offer your bodies as a living sacrifice, holy and pleasing to God—this is your true and proper worship. Do not conform to the pattern of this world, but be transformed by the renewing of your mind. Then you will be able to test and approve what God's will is—his good, pleasing and perfect will.*

Proverbs 3:1–6 (NIV) *My son, do not forget my teaching, but keep my commands in your heart, for they will prolong your life many years and bring you peace and prosperity. Let love and faithfulness never leave you; bind them around your neck, write them on the tablet of your heart. Then you will win favor and a good name in the sight of God and man.*

Trust in the Lord with all your heart and lean not on your own understanding; in all your ways submit to him, and he will make your paths straight.

Notes:

1. What stood out to you in the passages?
2. List three areas of your life in which you have difficulty surrendering to God:

    a.

    b.

    c.

3. Part of the Practice of Surrender and Trust includes submitting to the priorities of God's Kingdom and a commitment to walking in the Spirit. Now, in that last sentence, circle whichever of those areas is *most* difficult. Write out a brief prayer of surrender to God below, including one specific act of repentance.

    Father, I surrender...

 Journaling consists of keeping a personal record of your life experiences, faith journey, and reflections of the Bible.

Try journaling during the weeks until you meet again. Remember, there are no right or wrong ways to journal. The goal is simply to pay attention and record insights into the occurrences of your everyday life. Agree on one idea to journal about before you meet again:

1. Write about what you're learning (insights, wisdom, understanding, etc.).
2. Write down observations you make as you read Scripture. Record questions you're asking or things that are continually occupying your thoughts.
3. Write out your prayers. Consider using the ACTS acrostic in organizing your prayer:

    A—Adoration—Begin by expressing your adoration to God.
    C—Confession—Admit your wrongdoing.
    T—Thanksgiving—List what you're grateful for.
    S—Supplication—Ask God for help.

Try writing out a prayer using ACTS:

Discussion Prompts and Questions:

1. Review your responses to the Scriptures you've been reading. If you haven't read the Scripture prior to today, read it now and answer the questions together.
2. Discuss your thoughts regarding journaling. What benefits do you see in taking time to write down and record your thoughts?
3. What are you learning about living a life marked by Surrender and Trust? Share the one area of surrender you identified on your own and pray about this together.

Preparation for Your Third Meeting

Interacting with Scripture

John 12:24–26 (NIV) *Very truly I tell you, unless a kernel of wheat falls to the ground and dies, it remains only a single seed. But if it dies, it produces many seeds. Anyone who loves their life will lose it, while anyone who hates their life in this world will keep it for eternal life. Whoever serves me must follow me; and where I am, my servant also will be. My Father will honor the one who serves me.*

John 3:1–18 (NIV) *Now there was a Pharisee, a man named Nicodemus who was a member of the Jewish ruling council. He came to Jesus at night and said, "Rabbi, we know that you are a teacher who has come from God. For no one could perform the signs you are doing if God were not with him."*

Jesus replied, "Very truly I tell you, no one can see the kingdom of God unless they are born again.

Notes:

"How can someone be born when they are old?" Nicodemus asked. "Surely they cannot enter a second time into their mother's womb to be born!"

Jesus answered, "Very truly I tell you, no one can enter the kingdom of God unless they are born of water and the Spirit. Flesh gives birth to flesh, but the Spirit gives birth to spirit. You should not be surprised at my saying, 'You must be born again.' The wind blows wherever it pleases. You hear its sound, but you cannot tell where it comes from or where it is going. So it is with everyone born of the Spirit."

"How can this be?" Nicodemus asked.

"You are Israel's teacher," said Jesus, "and do you not understand these things? Very truly I tell you, we speak of what we know, and we testify to what we have seen, but still you people do not accept our testimony. I have spoken to you of earthly things and you do not believe; how then will you believe if I speak of heavenly things? No one has ever gone into heaven except the one who came from heaven—the Son of Man. Just as Moses lifted up the snake in the wilderness, so the Son of Man must be lifted up, that everyone who believes may have eternal life in him."

For God so loved the world that he gave his one and only Son, that whoever believes in him shall not perish but have eternal life. For God did not send his Son into the world to condemn the world, but to save the world through him. Whoever believes in him is not condemned, but whoever does not believe stands condemned already because they have not believed in the name of God's one and only Son.

Notes:

<u>Matthew 11:28–30 (NIV)</u> *"Come to me, all you who are weary and burdened, and I will give you rest. Take my yoke upon you and learn from me, for I am gentle and humble in heart, and you will find rest for your souls. For my yoke is easy and my burden is light."*

 ## Discussion Prompts and Questions:

1. What stood out to you in these passages?
2. In the Gospel of John, Jesus speaks of our need to die and to be born again. How have you experienced dying and rebirth in your own life?
3. Jesus is clear: we can't properly follow Him on our own; we must partner with His Holy Spirit in order to be transformed into the person He longs for us to be. How do you understand the role of the Holy Spirit in your life? How can you make walking in the Spirit a daily practice?

 Self-examination is the process of reflecting deeply on the state of one's soul, particularly one's conduct, motives and desires.

Set aside time to reflect on the following questions. Don't rush. You will gain the most from the discipline of self-examination if you return to the same question over several days or weeks. Choose one or two questions to process before your next meeting.

1. What do I desire to be true about my life and faith? What am I doing currently to move toward this? What's hindering me from getting there?
2. What has God been doing in my life in the past three to six months? What themes are emerging?
3. How am I responding to others? Do I react in my flesh or respond in the Spirit? Am I experiencing a reoccurring emotion?

Confession is an honest admission to God of ways you've sinned and your desire to repent.

Take time to confess any areas where you've hurt others or disobeyed God. Here are some suggestions to help you incorporate confession into your life. Read the examples below and choose one to try before your next meeting.

1. Make confession a regular part of your day. At the end of each day, take a few moments to reflect upon your day, asking the Holy Spirit to bring to mind any areas where you need to confess. Ask God to forgive you and help you to change.
2. Ask members of your family or close friends to help you see your blind spots. Ask questions like, "What do I do that hurts you? How could I better love you? What's it like to be with me? Do I show interest in others or talk mostly about myself?"[2] Let their answers guide you in a time of confession.
3. Imagine the kind of person you'd like to become in your old age. Then look at your life and assess whether or not the way you live now is preparing you to become that person. Confess where you need to change. Ask God and the community of faith to help.[3]
4. The seven deadly sins are vices that identify some of the darkest places of human nature, those places that may take the place of God in our lives. Prayerfully read through each of the seven vices. Allow the Spirit of God to bring conviction where appropriate, but don't give into condemnation. Journal your thoughts if you'd like.

---

2   Adele Ahlberg Calhoun, *Spiritual Disciplines Handbook: Practices That Transform Us*. Downers Grove: InterVarsity Press, 2005.

3   Ibid.

Vice	Description	Notes
Pride	Pride is understood to be the sin of Satan, expressed in his desire to be like God. Pride wants to focus attention anywhere but on its own sinfulness and does not concede that Christ has any authority to condemn our sinfulness.	
Envy	Envy is dissatisfaction with who God has made us to be. It's also suspicion that God is withholding what we deserve and giving it to someone else.	
Gluttony	Gluttony is the pursuit and overindulgence of the body's appetites, especially for food and drink.	
Lust	Lust has its root in the belief that God's love isn't enough to satisfy our longing for intimacy and seeks to fill that longing through visual and physical sexual sin.	
Anger	Anger that's inordinate or inappropriate (sinful) is directed at selfish and mundane matters. Sinful anger comes unbidden and in greater intensity than the situation warrants.	
Greed	Greed grows out of the suspicion that God won't take care of our needs as well as we can take care of ourselves. It's oriented toward material possessions, wanting the good things others have.	
Slothful	Being slothful is the neglect of the greatest commandment: to love the Lord your God with all your heart, soul, mind and strength. It's inattention to our spiritual lives, and failure to do anything that God asks of us or even simply what needs to be done.[1]	

4   Mindy Caliguire, *Soul Searching.* Downers Grove: InterVarsity Press, 2008.

Growing in the Practice of Surrender and Trust: At the beginning of this practice you assessed where you were at that time. Now assess where you are today.

1. Where have I seen the most movement?
2. Where do I have the most room for growth?

 Discussion Prompts and Questions:

1. Review your responses to the Scriptures you've been reading. If you haven't read the Scripture prior to today, read it now and answer the questions together.
2. Discuss your thoughts regarding the spiritual disciplines of self-examination and confession. Were these spiritual disciplines new to you?
3. What was the most difficult thing for you about these disciplines? How will you incorporate them into your life?

The Practice of Surrender and Trust—Summary

Discuss before moving on to the next essential practice:

1. What have you learned about the Practice of Surrender and Trust? Where have you seen the most movement? Where do you have the most room for growth?
2. In what areas of your life is God calling you to surrender and trust Him more?
3. Now that you've experimented with some of the accompanying spiritual disciplines, circle one you'll focus on in integrating into your life for the next thirty days:
   - **Baptism**
   - **Communion**
   - **Journaling**
   - **Self-examination**
   - **Confession**

As a reminder, some spiritual disciplines will be more natural for you, while others will require intentional practice. Over time, you'll find a rhythm that's appropriate to your life stage and spiritual needs.

The Practice of Communion with God

In solitude I make the frustrating discovery that often my mind keeps me flailing around rather than settling into the rest of God. I begin to notice all the ways my mind distracts me from the very thing my soul is longing for, the experience of rest, union and communion with God.

—Barton, Invitation to Solitude and Silence

Preparation for Your First Meeting

Prepare to engage in the Practice of Communion with God by reading each passage below a few times.

<u>Psalm 46:10 (NIV)</u> *He says, "Be still, and know that I am God; I will be exalted among the nations, I will be exalted in the earth."*

<u>Psalm 27:4 (NIV)</u> *One thing I ask from the Lord, this only do I seek: that I may dwell in the house of the Lord all the days of my life, to gaze on the beauty of the Lord and to seek him in his temple.*

<u>Psalm 1:1–3 (NIV)</u> *Blessed is the one who does not walk in step with the wicked or stand in the way that sinners take or sit in the company of mockers, but whose delight is in the law of the Lord, and who meditates on his law day and night. That person is like a tree planted by streams of water, which yields its fruit in season and whose leaf does not wither—whatever they do prospers.*

 ## Practice Overview

Read through the following definition of the Practice of Communion with God. Highlight or underline the words or phrases that stand out to you.

Ordinary disciples of Jesus Christ practice Communion with God.
As children of God, disciples of Jesus long to be in the presence of their Father. They seek the heart of God and His desires and purposes on a daily basis. They want to know Him, hear from Him, and just be with Him. Their desire and need for intimacy with God drives them to alter their lives. They create the time and the environment that allows communion with Him. Disciples of Jesus Christ know that their strength, sustenance, wisdom, and security—their very lives—are rooted in the sacred space of the presence of God.

When disciples of Jesus Christ disengage from their routines and distractions and intimately commune with God, their lives will radically change. Disciples of Jesus who commune with God regularly cultivate sensitivity to the leading of the Holy Spirit, responsiveness to God's Word, security in their identity as children of God, and confidence in exercising their spiritual authority. People around them sense God's presence in them and are drawn into God's presence through them.

 Personal Assessment:

I want to know God, not just know about Him.	Strongly Disagree ☐	Somewhat Disagree ☐	Somewhat Agree ☐	Strongly Agree ☐		
I make time and space to grow in intimacy with Him.	Almost Never ☐	Rarely ☐	Occasionally ☐	Frequently ☐	Consistently ☐	Not Sure ☐
I disengage from my distractions and routines in order to meet with God.	Almost Never ☐	Rarely ☐	Occasionally ☐	Frequently ☐	Consistently ☐	Not Sure ☐
I've cultivated a sensitivity to the Holy Spirit's leading.	Strongly Disagree ☐	Somewhat Disagree ☐	Somewhat Agree ☐	Strongly Agree ☐		
I've cultivated a responsiveness to His word.	Strongly Disagree ☐	Somewhat Disagree ☐	Somewhat Agree ☐	Strongly Agree ☐		

I have the confidence I need to exercise spiritual authority.	Strongly Disagree	Somewhat Disagree	Somewhat Agree	Strongly Agree
	☐	☐	☐	☐

 Discussion Prompts and Questions:

1. If someone asked you to describe what the Practice of Communion with God means, what would you say?
2. Give examples of what it's been like to practice communion with God throughout your life.
3. Share your initial assessment on this practice.
4. What's currently going on in your life that requires you to commune with God in deeper ways?

 Interacting with Scripture

<u>1 Kings 19:11–12 (NIV)</u> *The Lord said, "Go out and stand on the mountain in the presence of the Lord, for the Lord is about to pass by." Then a great and powerful wind tore the mountains apart and shattered the rocks before the Lord, but the Lord was not in the wind. After the wind there was an earthquake, but the Lord was not in the earthquake. After the earthquake came a fire, but the Lord was not in the fire. And after the fire came a gentle whisper.*

<u>Psalm 145:18 (NLT)</u> *The Lord is close to all who call on him, yes, to all who call on him in truth.*

<u>Psalm 70:4 (NLT)</u> *But may all who search for you be filled with joy and gladness in you. May those who love your salvation repeatedly shout, "God is great!"*

Notes:

1. What do these passages tell us about God's proximity to us?

45

2. God invites us to seek Him. How does the process of seeking God change you and your view of your circumstances?

Solitude is the one place where we can gain freedom from the forces of society that will otherwise relentlessly mold us.

—Ortberg, *The Life You've Always Wanted*

 Spiritual Disciplines

Over the next few weeks, you'll try some disciplines integral to developing the Practice of Communion with God:

- **Solitude and silence**
- **Breath prayers**
- **Devotional Bible reading (*Lectio Divina*)**
- **Sabbath**

 Solitude is the discipline of being alone, freeing ourselves from the distraction of people to give ourselves completely to God.

1. What physical place can you set aside for solitude?
2. What will you need to do to create this place? When would you use it?

 Silence is the discipline of unplugging from noise and words, stilling the mind and heart, and practicing the presence of being with God.

Silence deepens our experience of solitude, because in silence we choose to unplug not only from the constant stimulation of life in the company of others, but also from our own addiction to noise, words and activity.

—Barton, *Sacred Rhythms*

If you've never experimented with this discipline, try five minutes of it for several days in a row. While you practice Communion with God, also notice how you feel. Notice your distractions. They could be areas in your life you need to give over to God. Keep practicing and eventually add more time to your silent periods each day.

Preparation for Your Second Meeting

 ### Interacting with Scripture

Psalm 62:5–6 (MSG) *God, the one and only—I'll wait as long as He says. Everything I hope for comes from him, so why not? He's solid rock under my feet, breathing room for my soul, an impregnable castle: I'm set for life.*

Acts 17:27–28 (NIV) *God did this so that they would seek him and perhaps reach out for him and find him, though he is not far from any one of us. "For in him we live and move and have our being."*

Psalm 46:10 (NIV) *He says, "Be still, and know that I am God; I will be exalted among the nations, I will be exalted in the earth."*

Notes: _____

1. What stood out to you in the passages?
2. Where did you find "breathing room for your soul?" Did having a specific place help you in your practice of silence and solitude?
3. What were your struggles with solitude and silence? What surprised you?

I cannot transform myself, or anything else for that matter. What I can do is create the conditions in which spiritual transformation can take place, by developing and maintaining a rhythm of spiritual practices that keep me open and available to God.

—Barton, *Sacred Rhythms*

Discussion Prompts and Questions:

1. Review your responses to the Scriptures you've been reading. If you haven't read the Scripture prior to today, read it now and answer the questions together.
2. Describe your experience with solitude and silence. How did these disciplines help your communion with God?
3. What are you learning about living a life marked by communion with God? Share the struggles and/or surprises you faced with silence and solitude. Pray over these together.

 Breath Prayers are short prayers we utter frequently to refocus us on the constant presence of God.

Examples: "Lord Jesus, have mercy." "Thy kingdom come; Thy will be done." "Bless the Lord, oh my soul." Use one of these breath prayers or create your own. Try using it over the next week.

My breath prayer:

Preparation for Your Third Meeting

 Interacting with Scripture

Matthew 11:28–30 (MSG) *Are you tired? Worn out? Burned out on religion? Come to me. Get away with me and you'll recover your life. I'll show you how to take a real rest. Walk with me and work with me—watch how I do it. Learn the unforced rhythms of grace. I won't lay anything heavy or ill-fitting on you. Keep company with me and you'll learn to live freely and lightly.*

Notes:

<u>Exodus 14:13–14 (NIV)</u> *Moses answered the people, "Do not be afraid. Stand firm and you will see the deliverance the Lord will bring you today. The Egyptians you see today you will never see again. The Lord will fight for you; you need only to be still."*

1. What stood out to you in these passages?
2. In what ways are you "weary?" What burdens do you carry? Hand them over to Jesus. Allow Him to take that yoke from you and give you true rest.
3. In the Matthew 11:28-30 passage, what do you think Jesus means when He says to "learn the unforced rhythms of grace"? What is appealing about His invitation?

Two other disciplines related to this practice are Devotional Bible Reading and Sabbath:

> **Lectio Divina—How to read devotionally:**
>
> - Choose a short passage of Scripture (six verses or less).
> - Read it first audibly and slowly.
> - Read it again, this time listening for a word or phrase. Write it down.
> - Read it a third time, asking God why that word or phrase stood out.
> - Read it a final time, responding back to God through prayer.

 Devotional Bible Reading *(Lectio Divina,* Latin for sacred reading) is the repetitive, thoughtful reading and contemplation of Scripture passages with an attitude of surrender and openness.

It's less about gaining explicit knowledge and more about personal transformation. Go back to the Matthew 11:28–30 passage. Try approaching it with the method of devotional reading described on the right (*Lectio Divina*).

 Sabbath is a specific period of rest from the labors of life for the purpose of rejuvenation and fellowship with God and one another.

1. Evaluate the pace of your life. How might your current pace be affecting your soul and those around you?
2. What does real "rest" look like for you?
3. When do you set aside work or other routines in order to rest or reflect on God?

Growing in the Practice of Communion with God: At the beginning of this practice you assessed where you were at that time. Now assess where you are today.

1. Where have you seen the most movement?
2. Where do you see the most room for growth?

 Discussion Prompts and Questions:

1. Review your responses to the Scriptures you've been reading. If you haven't read the Scripture prior to today, read it now and answer the questions together.
2. What did you find the most difficult about practicing *Lectio Divina*? What did you discover about yourself, God, and His word?
3. How will you incorporate these various spiritual disciplines into your life?

The Practice of Communion with God—Summary

Discuss before moving on to the next essential practice:

1. What have you learned about the Practice of Communion with God? Where have you seen the most movement? Where do you have the most room for growth?
2. Now that you've experimented with some of the accompanying spiritual disciplines, circle at least one you'll integrate into your life:
     - **Solitude and silence**
     - **Breath prayers**
     - **Devotional Bible reading (*Lectio Divina*)**
     - **Sabbath**
3. How does the Practice of Communion with God relate to the Practice of Surrender and Trust?

   As a reminder, some spiritual disciplines will be more natural for you, while others will require intentional practice. Over time, you'll find a rhythm appropriate to your life stage and spiritual needs.

The Practice of Studying the Word of God

What we believe about the Bible: We believe the Bible was written by human authors under the supernatural inspiration of God and is our authority for all matters of faith and practice.

—Grace Church Statement of Belief

Preparation for Your First Meeting

Prepare to engage in the Practice of Studying the Word of God by reading each passage below a few times. Choose one to commit to memory over the next few weeks.

Psalm 19:7 (NIV) *The law of the Lord is perfect, ref reshing the soul. The statutes of the Lord are trustworthy, making wise the simple.*

Psalm 119:89 (NIV) *Your word, Lord, is eternal; it stands firm in the heavens.*

Deuteronomy 11:18–19 (NLT) *So commit yourselves wholeheartedly to these words of mine. Tie them to your hands and wear them on your forehead as reminders. Teach them to your children. Talk about them when you are at home and when you are on the road, when you are going to bed and when you are getting up.*

 Practice Overview

Read through the following definition of the Practice of Studying the Word of God. Highlight or underline the words or phrases that stand out to you.

Ordinary disciples of Jesus Christ study the Word of God and take in good Biblical teaching that will transform their lives.

Disciples of Jesus are readers and learners. They regularly subject their minds and hearts to the Bible, developing working knowledge of the Scriptures. Followers of Christ believe the Bible speaks to all aspects of life. In addition, ordinary disciples, hungry to know more about God and the Bible, expose themselves to other writings and teaching that help shape their understanding of God, His purposes, their world, and themselves.

Ordinary followers of Jesus who study the Word of God and take in good Biblical teaching will experience renewed minds, and their lifestyles will be constantly modified. As they read the Bible and let the Bible impact them, they begin to bear fruit and the dead wood of their lives is trimmed away. The more they read and learn, the more they'll know God. Convinced of its importance, ordinary disciples freely pass on their passion for the Word of God to the next generation.

1. How do you think popular culture views the Bible?
2. What do the passages in the introduction of this practice say about the Bible?
3. How would you defend the belief that the Bible is truly God's message to you?

 Personal Assessment:

I believe the Bible speaks to all areas of my life.	True ☐		Not True ☐		Not Sure ☐

I'm hungry to know about God and know God more through reading of the Bible.	True ☐		Not True ☐		Not Sure ☐

	Almost Never	Rarely	Occasionally	Frequently	Consistently	Not Sure
I intentionally read/listen to the Bible on my own.	☐	☐	☐	☐	☐	☐
I intentionally read Scripture and engage in conversations about the Bible with others.	☐	☐	☐	☐	☐	☐

I intentionally engage the next generation in the Bible (children, students, younger acquaintances, etc.).	Almost Never	Rarely	Occasionally	Frequently	Consistently	Not Sure
	☐	☐	☐	☐	☐	☐

 ## Discussion Prompts and Questions:

1. What key words did you highlight in the definition of this practice?
2. What did you learn about the Bible's credibility, authority, inspiration and intent from the passages you read?
3. What makes studying the Word of God a foundational practice for an ordinary disciple of Jesus?
4. Share your initial assessment on this practice with one another.

 ## Interacting with Scripture

2 Timothy 3:16–17 (NLT) *All Scripture is inspired by God and is useful to teach us what is true and to make us realize what is wrong in our lives. It corrects us when we are wrong and teaches us to do what is right. God uses it to prepare and equip his people to do every good work.*

Psalm 19:7 (NLT) *The instructions of the Lord are perfect, reviving the soul. The decrees of the Lord are trustworthy, making wise the simple.*

John 20:30–31 (NIV) *Jesus performed many other signs in the presence of his disciples, which are not recorded in this book. But these are written that you may believe that Jesus is the Messiah, the Son of God, and that by believing you may have life in his name.*

Notes:

Joshua 1:8 (NLT) *Study this Book of Instruction continually. Meditate on it day and night so you will be sure to obey everything written in it. Only then will you prosper and succeed in all you do.*

Notes:

Psalm 1:1–3 (MSG) *How well God must like you...you thrill to God's Word, you chew on Scripture day and night. You're a tree replanted in Eden, bearing fresh fruit every month, never dropping a leaf, always in blossom.*

John 17:17 (NIV) *Sanctify them by the truth; your word is truth.*

1. What do these verses tell you about the Bible's credibility?
2. What are some ways the Bible gives you a firm foundation on which to stand for life?
3. What do you learn about the Bible's authority, inspiration and intent?

Preparation for Your Second Meeting

 ### Interacting with Scripture

Psalm 119:1–8 (NLT) *Joyful are people of integrity, who follow the instructions of the L_ORD_. Joyful are those who obey his laws and search for him with all their hearts. They do not compromise with evil, and they walk only in his paths. You have charged us to keep your commandments carefully. Oh, that my actions would consistently reflect your decrees! Then I will not be ashamed when I compare my life with your commands. As I learn your righteous regulations, I will thank you by living as I should! I will obey your decrees. Please don't give up on me!*

Notes:

1. What about God's Word brings the psalmist joy and thanksgiving?
2. What's the author's overall posture toward studying the Word of God?
3. How can you apply this posture toward your Bible reading?

Spiritual Disciplines

Over the next few weeks, you'll try some disciplines integral in developing the Practice of Studying the Word of God:

- **Memorization**
- **Devotional Bible reading**
- **Journaling**
- **Inductive Bible study**
- **Studying the Word of God in community**

 Memorization is a careful, repetitive meditation on certain passages of Scripture so as to set them to memory and have them available to recall at any time as you respond to life circumstances.

Consider the passage you memorized in the "Getting Started" section. Answer the following questions:

1. What did you experience in the memorization process?
2. What insights have you drawn from this passage?
3. How might memorization help you respond to life circumstances?

Before your next meeting, memorize Proverbs 3:5–6.

 Devotional Bible Reading *Lectio Divina* (Latin for sacred reading) is the repetitive, thoughtful reading and contemplation of Scripture passages with an attitude of surrender and openness.

Read Psalm 1 and journal your thoughts using the discipline of *Lectio Divina*:
1. Read the passage audibly and slowly.
2. Read the passage again, this time listening for a word or phrase. Write it down.

3. Read the passage a third time, asking God to help you understand why that word or phrase stood out to you.

4. Read the passage a final time, responding back to God through prayer.

 ## Interacting with Scripture

<u>Psalm 1:1–6 (NIV)</u> *Blessed is the one who does not walk in step with the wicked or stand in the way that sinners take or sit in the company of mockers, but whose delight is in the law of the Lord, and who meditates on his law day and night. That person is like a tree planted by streams of water, which yields its fruit in season and whose leaf does not wither—whatever they do prospers.*

Not so the wicked! They are like chaff that the wind blows away. Therefore the wicked will not stand in the judgment, nor sinners in the assembly of the righteous. For the Lord watches over the way of the righteous, but the way of the wicked leads to destruction.

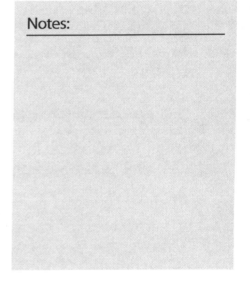

Notes:

 Journaling consists of keeping a personal record of your life experiences, faith journey, and reflections of the Bible.

Next time you meet, take your journal to discuss your experience with daily devotional reading. Your journal can be as simple as a ruled notebook.

Discussion Prompts and Questions:

1. Describe your experience with the Practice of Lectio Divina. What words, phrases, or ideas stood out to you in Psalm 1?
2. What did you sense God was saying to you through this passage?
3. At this stage of your spiritual journey, what do you need to change in order to make devotional Bible reading a regular practice? Pray together, asking God to help you make the necessary changes.

Inductive Bible Study involves reading a book of the Bible and studying the history and context of the story while also determining how that story might apply to us today.

Note: In the Resources section in the back of this book there is a guide to Inductive Bible Study.

Here are a few of the questions you might ask with Inductive Bible Study:
1. Who's the writer, and who's the recipient?
2. What's the book about?
3. When was the book written?
4. Why was the book written?
5. What's the context of this passage?
6. What's God saying in this passage?
7. How might you respond to what you've learned?

Practice Inductive Bible Study by reading the book of James and researching the answer to questions about the author, purpose for the book, context in the New Testament, and what it says to you today.

1. What did you learn about the story and context of this book?
2. What's God saying to you through the book of James?

Growing in the Practice of Studying the Word of God: At the beginning of this practice you assessed where you were at that time. Now assess where you are today

1. Where have I seen the most movement?
2. Where do I have the most room for growth?

Preparation for Your Third Meeting

 Interacting with Scripture

To make studying the Word of God a regular practice, read the Bible every day. Find a quiet place and ask God to speak to you. Commit to reading the book of Luke. Start by using your online resources to learn the history and context of the book. Then devotionally read a chapter of Luke each day for the next twenty-four days. Listen for Jesus to teach you His ways as He taught His disciples. As you read each chapter, circle key words that stand out to you and journal your answers to these questions:

1. What did I notice was important to Jesus?
2. What sort of questions does He ask people?
3. What sort of questions do people ask Him?
4. What's He inviting me to be, as a follower of Jesus? What's He inviting me to do?

Journal your reflections each day and share them the next time you meet.

 Studying the Word of God in community is discussing the Bible and learning with others in a small group.

1. Beyond this discipleship relationship, discuss your engagement in studying the Word of God in community.
2. What would need to change for you to make this a regular discipline?

Growing in the Practice of Studying the Word of God: At the beginning of this practice you assessed where you were at that time. Now assess where you are today.

1. Where have I seen the most movement?
2. Where do I have the most room for growth?

 Discussion Prompts and Questions:

1. Review your responses to the Scriptures you've been reading. If you haven't read the Scripture prior to today, read it now and answer the questions together.
2. Discuss your thoughts regarding the spiritual disciplines of studying the Word of God on your own and in community.
3. What was the most difficult thing for you about these disciplines? How will you incorporate them into your life?

The Practice of Studying the Word of God—Summary

Discuss before moving on to the next essential practice:

1. What have you learned about the Practice of Studying the Word of God? Where have you seen the most movement? Where do you have the most room for growth? How does this practice relate to Surrender and Trust and/or communion with God?
2. Now that you've experimented with some of the accompanying spiritual disciplines, circle at least one you'll integrate into your life:
   - **Memorization**
   - **Devotional Bible Reading**
   - **Journaling**
   - **Inductive Bible Study**
   - **Studying the Word of God in Community**

As a reminder, some spiritual disciplines will be more natural for you, while others will require intentional practice. Over time, you'll find a rhythm that's appropriate to your life stage and spiritual needs.

Practices That Provide Stability

The Practice of Self-Denial

> Cheap grace is the grace we bestow on ourselves. Cheap grace is the preaching of forgiveness without requiring repentance, baptism without church discipline, communion without confession...Cheap grace is grace without discipleship, grace without the cross, grace without Jesus Christ, living and incarnate.
>
> —Bonhoeffer, The Cost of Discipleship

Preparation for Your First Meeting

Prepare to engage in the Practice of Self-Denial by reading each passage below a few times. Choose one to commit to memory over the next few weeks.

<u>1 John 2:6 (NIV)</u> *Whoever claims to live in him must live as Jesus did.*

<u>1 Peter 4:1–2 (NIV)</u> *Therefore, since Christ suffered in his body, arm yourselves also with the same attitude, because he who has suffered in his body is done with sin. As a result, he does not live the rest of his earthly life for evil human desires, but rather for the will of God.*

<u>Galatians 5:22–25 (NIV)</u> *But the fruit of the Spirit is love, joy, peace, forbearance, kindness, goodness, faithfulness, gentleness and self-control. Against such things there is no law. Those who belong to Christ Jesus have crucified the flesh with its passions and desires. Since we live by the Spirit, let us keep in step with the Spirit.*

 ## Practice Overview

Read through the following definition of the Practice of Self-Denial. Highlight or underline the words or phrases that stand out to you.

Ordinary disciples of Jesus Christ practice Self-Denial.

Jesus calls those who follow Him to live in complete and daily abandonment of personal agendas and self-centered desires. He asks disciples to make His kingdom purposes the priority of their lives. Jesus went so far as to say that those who die to themselves and lose their lives for His sake won't only have their needs provided but will find real life in the process. Jesus intended the Practice of Self-Denial not to be only the lifestyle of a few monastic recluses but to be the normal way for every Christian disciple. It's the way Jesus lived, and it's the way He expects us to live.

When disciples of Jesus Christ willingly live counter culturally by practicing disciplines of self-denial, they experience the fruit of love, joy, peace, patience, kindness, goodness, faithfulness, gentleness, and self-control. They're no longer burdened and powerless under their sinful, destructive desires, but they're singularly focused on God's kingdom and His purposes.

 Personal Assessment:

	Almost Never	Rarely	Occasionally	Frequently	Consistently	Not Sure
I live in complete and daily abandonment of my personal agendas and self-centered ideas.	☐	☐	☐	☐	☐	☐
I live daily with God's kingdom purposes as the number one priority of my life.	☐	☐	☐	☐	☐	☐
I live counter culturally by intentionally denying myself for Christ's sake.	☐	☐	☐	☐	☐	☐
I experience the fruit of the Holy Spirit as I live focused on God and His kingdom purposes rather than my own sinful desires.	☐	☐	☐	☐	☐	☐

Record any places in your life you tend to be overly concerned with your own needs, comfort and image:

Discussion Prompts and Questions:

1. If someone were to ask you to describe what the Practice of Self-Denial means, what would you say?
2. Who in your life has best modeled self-denial? Share anything you've learned about this practice from watching others.
3. Share your initial assessment on this practice.
4. In what area(s) of your life have you chosen to follow your own agenda and desires rather than denying yourself for God's purposes?

Interacting with Scripture

Philippians 2:3–8 (NIV) *Do nothing out of selfish ambition or vain conceit. Rather, in humility value others above yourselves, not looking to your own interests but each of you to the interests of the others. In your relationships with one another, have the same mindset as Christ Jesus: Who, being in very nature God, did not consider equality with God something to be used to his own advantage; rather, he made himself nothing by taking the very nature of a servant, being made in human likeness. And being found in appearance as a man, he humbled himself by becoming obedient to death—even death on a cross!*

Mark 10:35–45 (NIV) *Then James and John, the sons of Zebedee, came to him. "Teacher," they said, "we want you to do for us whatever we ask." "What do you want me to do for you?" he asked. They replied, "Let one of us sit at your right and the other at your left in your glory." "You don't know what you are asking," Jesus said. "Can you drink the cup I drink or be baptized with the baptism I am baptized with?" "We can," they answered. Jesus said to them, "You*

Notes:

will drink the cup I drink and be baptized with the baptism I am baptized with, but to sit at my right or left is not for me to grant. These places belong to those for whom they have been prepared." When the ten heard about this, they became indignant with James and John. Jesus called them together and said, "You know that those who are regarded as rulers of the Gentiles lord it over them, and their high officials exercise authority over them. Not so with you. Instead, whoever wants to become great among you must be your servant, and whoever wants to be first must be slave of all. For even the Son of Man did not come to be served, but to serve, and to give his life as a ransom for many."

Notes:

1. What do these passages suggest about self-denial?
2. Write here about a recent time when you placed the needs of someone else above your own.
3. Revisit a specific time or situation in your life where you tended toward selfish ambition. How could you have responded differently?

Without rest, we miss the rest of God: the rest that He invites us to enter more fully so that we might know Him more deeply.

—Buchanan, *Your God Is Too Safe*

 ## Spiritual Disciplines

Over the next few weeks, you'll try some disciplines integral in developing the Practice of Self-Denial:

- **Sabbath**
- **Simplicity**
- **Abstinence**
- **Fasting**

Sabbath is a specific period of rest from the labors of life for the purpose of rejuvenation and fellowship with God and one another.

 ### Interacting with Scripture

<u>Isaiah 58:13–14 (NIV)</u> *"If you keep your feet from breaking the Sabbath and from doing as you please on my holy day, if you call the Sabbath a delight and the LORD's holy day honorable, and if you honor it by not going your own way and not doing as you please or speaking idle words, then you will find your joy in the LORD, and I will cause you to ride on the heights of the land and to feast on the inheritance of your father Jacob." The mouth of the LORD has spoken.*

Notes:

<u>Psalm 23:1–3 (NIV)</u> *The LORD is my Shepherd, I shall not be in want. He makes me lie down in green pastures, he leads me beside quiet waters, He restores my soul.*

1.   How do you currently practice Sabbath?
2.   What keeps you from practicing Sabbath?

Sabbath-keeping honors the body's need for rest, the spirit's need for replenishment and the soul's need to delight itself in God for god's own sake.

—Barton, *Invitation to Solitude and Silence*

Put a date on your calendar for a Sabbath at some point over the next thirty days. Ask God to help you choose activities that day that will replenish your spirit and restore your soul (a nap, reading, prayer, listening to music, a long walk, etc.). Ask God to also show you what activities you might eliminate that day. Record your thoughts below:

By living a deeply reduced life we hoped to discover a greatly increased God.

—Hatmaker, *7: An Experimental Mutiny against Excess*

Preparation for Your Second Meeting

 ## Interacting with Scripture

<u>Matthew 6:25–34 (NIV)</u> *Therefore I tell you, do not worry about your life, what you will eat or drink; or about your body, what you will wear. Is not life more important than food, and the body more important than clothes?*

Look at the birds of the air; they do not sow or reap or store away in barns, and yet your heavenly Father feeds them. Are you not much more valuable than they? Who of you by worrying can add a single hour to his life? "And why do you worry about clothes? See how the lilies of the field grow. They do not labor or spin. Yet I tell you that not even Solomon in all his splendor was dressed like one of these.

If that's how God clothes the grass of the field, which is here today and tomorrow is thrown into the fire, will he not much more clothe you, O you of little faith?

So do not worry, saying, 'What shall we eat?' or 'What shall we drink?' or 'What shall we wear?' For the pagans run after all these things, and your heavenly Father knows that you need them. But seek first his kingdom and his righteousness, and all these things will be given to you as well.

Therefore do not worry about tomorrow, for tomorrow will worry about itself. Each day has enough trouble of its own.

Notes:
_____

Luke 9:23–25 (NIV) *Then he said to them all: "If anyone would come after me, he must deny himself and take up his cross daily and follow me. For whoever wants to save his life will lose it, but whoever loses his life for me will save it. What good is it for a man to gain the whole world, and yet lose or forfeit his very self?*

Notes:

1. What stood out to you in these passages?
2. List three specific things you tend to hold on to, either concerned you need more of them or convinced you don't have enough.
3. What might "denying yourself daily in order to follow Christ" look like?

 Simplicity is the choice to scale down the consumption and busyness of life, living purposely with less, and choosing to do less.

The following exercise will help you take inventory, paying attention to areas in your life you might be able to reduce or simplify.

Count the following:

_____ number of items of clothing or shoes in your closet

_____ number of hours you spend on e-mail, texts, Facebook, Twitter, Pinterest, etc. per day

_____ number of items you have in your pantry, refrigerator, or freezer

_____ number of media/technology items in your home

_____ number of purchases you've made in the last month

_____ number of places you've purchased items in the last month

Ask God to reveal your abundance. Where do you see excess or more than you need?

 Discussion Prompts and Questions:

1. Review your responses to the Scriptures you've been reading. If you haven't read the Scripture prior to today, read it now and answer the questions together.

2. Discuss your thoughts regarding Sabbath. Did you make plans to put a Sabbath on your calendar? If you've already practiced Sabbath since your last meeting, share your experience. If not, make a plan now to incorporate Sabbath in your life sometime over the next thirty days.

3. How might you incorporate simplicity into your life? What regular activity might you release going forward to live more simplistically?

4. How did you respond to the inventory-taking exercise? Where did you notice places you have more than you need?

You can't read the Bible very far in any direction without realizing that fasting was simply a part of the natural rhythm of life for the people of God.

—Buchanan, Your God Is Too Safe

Preparation for Your Third Meeting

 ### Interacting with Scripture

<u>Ephesians 4:17–32 (NLT)</u> *With the Lord's authority I say this: Live no longer as the Gentiles do, for they are hopelessly confused. Their minds are full of darkness; they wander far from the life God gives because they have closed their minds and hardened their hearts against him. They have no sense of shame. They live for lustful pleasure and eagerly practice every kind of impurity. But that isn't what you learned about Christ. Since you have heard about Jesus and have learned the truth that comes from him, throw off your old sinful nature and your former way of life, which is corrupted by lust and deception. Instead, let the Spirit renew your thoughts and attitudes. Put on your new nature, created to be like God—truly righteous and holy. So stop telling lies. Let us tell our neighbors the truth, for we are all parts of the same body. And "don't sin by letting anger control you." Don't let the sun go down while you are still angry, for anger gives a foothold to the devil.*

Notes:

If you are a thief, quit stealing. Instead, use your hands for good hard work, and then give generously to others in need. Don't use foul or abusive language. Let everything you say be good and helpful, so that your words will be an encouragement to those who hear them.

And do not bring sorrow to God's Holy Spirit by the way you live. Remember, he has identified you as his own, guaranteeing that you will be saved on the day of redemption.

Get rid of all bitterness, rage, anger, harsh words, and slander, as well as all types of evil behavior. Instead, be kind to each other, tenderhearted, forgiving one another, just as God through Christ has forgiven you.

<u>1 Peter 2:11–12 (NIV)</u> *Dear friends, I urge you, as aliens and strangers in the world, to abstain from sinful desires, which war against your soul. Live such good lives among the pagans that, though they accuse you of doing wrong, they may see your good deeds and glorify God on the day he visits us.*

Notes:

1. What stood out to you in these passages?
2. Circle any words or phrases in the above passages that you suspect may currently characterize your habits or lifestyle. Ask God for humility to see these patterns in your life.

 Abstinence is a longer form of fasting through avoidance of any specific thing, such as alcoholic beverages, meat, or sexual activity, with the intent of focusing on a godly life.

What practical steps can you take to move away from those things that may be hindering your Godly living? Write a prayer to God, asking for His help as you work to abstain from these things.

THE WAY OF DISCIPLESHIP

 ## Interacting with Scripture

<u>Deuteronomy 8:1–17 (NIV)</u> *Be careful to follow every command I am giving you today, so that you may live and increase and may enter and possess the land that the LORD promised on oath to your forefathers. Remember how the LORD your God led you all the way in the desert these forty years, to humble you and to test you in order to know what was in your heart, whether or not you would keep his commands.*

He humbled you, causing you to hunger and then feeding you with manna, which neither you nor your fathers had known, to teach you that man does not live on bread alone but on every word that comes from the mouth of the LORD. Your clothes did not wear out and your feet did not swell during these forty years. Know then in your heart that as a man disciplines his son, so the LORD your God disciplines you. Observe the commands of the LORD your God, walking in his ways and revering him.

For the LORD your God is bringing you into a good land—a land with streams and pools of water, with springs flowing in the valleys and hills; a land with wheat and barley, vines and fig trees, pomegranates, olive oil and honey; a land where bread will not be scarce and you will lack nothing; a land where the rocks are iron and you can dig copper out of the hills. When you have eaten and are satisfied, praise the LORD your God for the good land he has given you.

Be careful that you do not forget the LORD your God, failing to observe his commands, his laws and his decrees that I am giving you this day. Otherwise, when you eat and are

Notes:

THE PRACTICE OF SELF-DENIAL

satisfied, when you build fine houses and settle down, and when your herds and flocks grow large and your silver and gold increase and all you have is multiplied, then your heart will become proud and you will forget the LORD your God, who brought you out of Egypt, out of the land of slavery.

He led you through the vast and dreadful desert, that thirsty and waterless land, with its venomous snakes and scorpions. He brought you water out of hard rock. He gave you manna to eat in the desert, something your fathers had never known, to humble and to test you so that in the end it might go well with you. You may say to yourself, "My power and the strength of my hands have produced this wealth for me."

Notes:

1. What stood out to you in these passages?
2. What does God warn about living in excess?

 Fasting is temporarily abstaining from eating food (or electronic media, television, etc.) for a period of time with the purpose of focusing on prayer and spiritual guidance.

This week, consider what you might be able to fast. Choosing to miss a meal is the most common way to fast but is only one of many options. Here are some other ideas you could choose.

dessert	dining out	Twitter
watching a particular television show	shopping	Facebook
reading	using the Internet	a comfort food/beverage
texting	talking on the phone	other entertainment

Growing in the Practice of Self-Denial: At the beginning of this practice, you assessed where you were at that time. Now assess where you are today.

1. Where have I seen the most movement?
2. Where do I have the most room for growth?

 Discussion Prompts and Questions:

1. Review your responses to the Scriptures you've been reading. If you haven't read the Scripture prior to today, read it now and answer the questions together.
2. Discuss your thoughts regarding the spiritual disciplines of abstinence and fasting. Were these spiritual disciplines new to you?
3. How does this practice relate to Surrender and Trust?
4. What was the most difficult thing for you about these disciplines? How will you incorporate them into your life?

The Practice of Self-Denial—Summary

Discuss before moving on to the next essential practice:

1. What have you learned about the Practice of Self-Denial? Where have you seen the most movement? Where do you have the most room for growth?
2. In what areas of your life is God calling you toward self-denial?
3. Now that you've experimented with some of the accompanying spiritual disciplines, circle one you will focus on in the next thirty days to integrate into your life:
   - **Sabbath**
   - **Simplicity**
   - **Abstinence**
   - **Fasting**

As a reminder, some spiritual disciplines will be more natural for you, while others will require intentional practice. Over time, you'll find a rhythm that's appropriate to your life stage and spiritual needs.

The Practice of Moral Integrity

> All of us can grow in the kinds of real character that bring about fruitful re-
> lationships and achievement of purpose, mission, and goals. Integrity is not
> something that you either have or don't, but instead is an exciting growth
> path that all of us can engage in and enjoy.
>
> —Cloud, Integrity

Preparation for Your First Meeting

Engage in the following Scripture and disciplines:

<u>Ephesians 4:22–24 (NIV)</u> *You were taught, with regard to your former way of life, to put off your old self, which is being corrupted by its deceitful desires; to be made new in the attitude of your minds; and to put on the new self, created to be like God in true righteousness and holiness.*

<u>Romans 6:13–14 (NIV)</u> *Do not offer any part of yourself to sin as an instrument of wickedness, but rather offer yourselves to God as those who have been brought from death to life; and offer every part of yourself to him as an instrument of righteousness. For sin shall no longer be your master, because you are not under the law, but under grace.*

 Practice Overview

Read through the following definition of the Practice of Moral Integrity. Highlight or underline the words or phrases that stand out to you.

Ordinary disciples of Jesus Christ practice Moral Integrity.

Followers of Christ are urged to live lives worthy of their callings. God has redeemed His children from their formerly empty lives characterized by darkness, ignorance, and impurity. Disciples are now empowered by His Spirit and commanded to be holy as God is holy. Ordinary disciples of Jesus are committed to obedience to the commands and principles of God's Word. They're expected to live according to the Spirit rather than their old sinful natures. As God's holy people, there's not to be even a hint of immorality among them. The calling of living as God's chosen people in this world is a high calling and is to be accompanied by a moral life in keeping with that calling.

When Jesus' disciples live moral, holy lives, they honor their Father who's holy and show the world around them an example of a life of integrity. They're credible witnesses to the power of the Gospel. Perhaps the most important result of Christ followers practicing moral integrity is that future generations, their children and grandchildren, will have authentic examples to follow as they also learn to follow Jesus.

 Personal Assessment:

	True		Not True		Not Sure
I'm redeemed from my former empty way of life through Jesus Christ.	☐		☐		☐

	Almost Never	Rarely	Occasionally	Frequently	Consistently	Not Sure
I'm living a life worthy of my calling as a Christ follower.	☐	☐	☐	☐	☐	☐
My life is a credible witness of the Gospel.	☐	☐	☐	☐	☐	☐
I'm providing an authentic example to follow to leave a lasting legacy for future generations.	☐	☐	☐	☐	☐	☐

Discussion Prompts and Questions:

1. If someone were to ask you to describe what the Practice of Moral Integrity means, what would you say?
2. Why is the Practice of Moral Integrity essential to a follower of Jesus Christ?
3. Share your initial assessment on this practice.
4. Why do you suppose so many Christ followers struggle to live lives of moral integrity?

 ## Interacting with Scripture

Romans 6:1–14 (NIV) *What shall we say, then? Shall we go on sinning so that grace may increase? By no means! We are those who have died to sin; how can we live in it any longer? Or don't you know that all of us who were baptized into Christ Jesus were baptized into his death? We were therefore buried with him through baptism into death in order that, just as Christ was raised from the dead through the glory of the Father, we too may live a new life.*

For if we have been united with him in a death like his, we will certainly also be united with him in a resurrection like his. For we know that our old self was crucified with him so that the body ruled by sin might be done away with, that we should no longer be slaves to sin—because anyone who has died has been set free from sin.

Now if we died with Christ, we believe that we will also live with him. For we know that since Christ was raised from the dead, he cannot die again; death no longer has mastery over him. The death he died, he died to sin once for all; but the life he lives, he lives to God.

Notes:

In the same way, count yourselves dead to sin but alive to God in Christ Jesus. Therefore do not let sin reign in your mortal body so that you obey its evil desires. Do not offer any part of yourself to sin as an instrument of wickedness, but rather offer yourselves to God as those who have been brought from death to life; and offer every part of yourself to him as an instrument of righteousness. For sin shall no longer be your master, because you are not under the law, but under grace.

Romans 8:9–13 (NIV) *You, however, are not in the realm of the flesh but are in the realm of the Spirit, if indeed the Spirit of God lives in you. And if anyone does not have the Spirit of Christ, they do not belong to Christ. But if Christ is in you, then even though your body is subject to death because of sin, the Spirit gives life because of righteousness. And if the Spirit of him who raised Jesus from the dead is living in you, he who raised Christ from the dead will also give life to your mortal bodies because of his Spirit who lives in you.*

Therefore, brothers and sisters, we have an obligation—but it is not to the flesh, to live according to it. For if you live according to the flesh, you will die; but if by the Spirit you put to death the misdeeds of the body, you will live.

Notes:

1. What do these passages tell us about God's view of moral integrity?
2. How would you describe the relationship between moral integrity and our identities as Christ followers?

Spiritual Disciplines Over the next few weeks, you'll try two disciplines integral in developing the Practice of Moral Integrity:

- **Studying the Bible and apologetics**
- **Journaling**
- **Accountability**
- **Vows of faithfulness or chastity**
- **Breath prayers**

 Studying the Bible and apologetics involves taking time to understand what we believe and why, so as to be able to convey this to others.

Through the Scriptures we learn what holiness and moral integrity look like from God's perspective.

Character, a wise person once said, is what we do when no one is looking. It is not the same as reputation—what other people think of us. It is not the same as success or achievement. Character is not what we have done, but who we are. And although we often hear of tragic lapses of character, describing its absence does not tell the whole story.

—Hybels, *Who You Are when No One's Looking*

Preparation for Your Second Meeting

 Interacting with Scripture

Ephesians 4:1–6 (NIV) *As a prisoner for the Lord, then, I urge you to live a life worthy of the calling you have received. Be completely humble and gentle; be patient, bearing with one another in love. Make every effort to keep the unity of the Spirit through the bond of peace. There is one body and one Spirit, just as you were called to one hope when you were*

Notes:

called; one Lord, one faith, one baptism; one God and Father of all, who is over all and through all and in all.

Notes:

Ephesians 5:1–2 (NIV) *Follow God's example, therefore, as dearly loved children and walk in the way of love, just as Christ loved us and gave himself up for us as a fragrant offering and sacrifice to God.*

2 Corinthians 5:20 (NIV) *We are therefore Christ's ambassadors, as though God were making his appeal through us. We implore you on Christ's behalf: Be reconciled to God.*

1 Thessalonians 2:14 (NIV) *For you, brothers and sisters, became imitators of God's churches in Judea, which are in Christ Jesus: You suffered from your own people the same things those churches suffered from the Jews.*

1. What stood out to you in these passages?
2. How do the following instructions from these scriptures challenge you?

   "Live a life worthy of the calling you received"
   "Follow God's example"
   "We are therefore Christ's ambassadors"
   "For you...became imitators of God's churches"
3. Whether familial or spiritual, what kind of legacy do you want to leave to future generations?

Each of these passages reminds us that when we live with moral integrity, we provide credibility to the message of Christ, "practicing what we preach." Ask God how credible your message is, based on how you live your life. Use this as another opportunity for confession, repentance, and resting in His forgiveness.

Discussion Prompts and Questions:

1. Review your responses to the Scriptures you've been reading. If you haven't read the Scripture prior to today, read it now and answer the questions together.

2. Too often people today are skeptical of the message of the Gospel because they're skeptical of Christians. Although many Christians claim the truths of the Bible, their everyday living doesn't represent that of a Christ follower. In fact, it discredits it. This creates a *credibility gap*. Nonbelievers aren't the least bit interested in pursuing a god whose followers say one thing and do another. In addition to a *credibility gap*, there's also a *sin gap*, which lies between sinful man and a holy God. While only Christ can bridge the sin gap, God uses you to bridge the credibility gap.

You   **Christ**

Credibility gap   **Sin Gap**

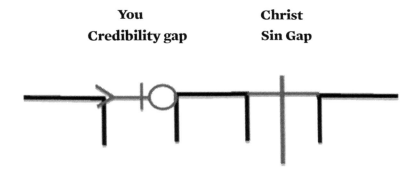

3. How do you see the credibility gap in our culture affecting our message regarding the sin gap?

4. Who has helped close the credibility gap for you? Briefly describe how this person helped you see Jesus and His claims more clearly.

5. Now think about your neighbors, friends and co-workers who are far from God. Would you say you are helping or hurting to bridge the credibility gap? If so, how? If not, what steps might you take to bridge the gap?

Preparation for Your Third Meeting

 Interacting with Scripture

<u>Galatians 5:19–25 (NIV)</u> *The acts of the flesh are obvious: sexual immorality, impurity and debauchery; idolatry and witchcraft; hatred, discord, jealousy, fits of rage, selfish ambition, dissensions, factions and envy; drunkenness, orgies, and the like. I warn you, as I did before, that those who live like this will not inherit the kingdom of God.*

But the fruit of the Spirit is love, joy, peace, forbearance, kindness, goodness, faithfulness, gentleness and self-control. Against such things there is no law. Those who belong to Christ Jesus have crucified the flesh with its passions and desires. Since we live by the Spirit, let us keep in step with the Spirit.

<u>Colossians 3:5–10 (NIV)</u> *Put to death, therefore, whatever belongs to your earthly nature: sexual immorality, impurity, lust, evil desires and greed, which is idolatry. Because of these, the wrath of God is coming. You used to walk in these ways, in the life you once lived. But now you must also rid yourselves of all such things as these: anger, rage, malice, slander, and filthy language from your lips. Do not lie to each other, since you have taken off your old self with its practices and have put on the new self, which is being renewed in knowledge in the image of its Creator.*

Notes: _____

1. What stood out to you in the passages?
2. Circle the various "acts of flesh" or "earthly nature" mentioned in the passage.
3. What particular "acts of the flesh" or things that belong to your "earthly nature" do you find yourself struggling to overcome?

Journaling consists of keeping a personal record of your life experiences, faith journey, and reflections of the Bible.

1. Write down the one act of the flesh you believe to be your biggest stumbling block. Be honest before God. Confess your sin. Repent. Accept His forgiveness. Ask the Holy Spirit for help going forward.
2. Keep a record of how you're doing in this area each day until you next meet with your discipler. Note any patterns you observe.

 Accountability is resolving to engage in relationships with others for the purposes of providing an honest perspective and rebuke, when necessary.

 Discussion Prompts and Questions:

1. Review your responses to the Scriptures you've been reading. If you haven't read the Scripture prior to today, read it now and answer the questions together.
2. Take a risk and share your biggest stumbling block in light of these words from James 5:16, 19–20 (NLT) Confess your sins to each other and pray for each other so that you may be healed. The earnest prayer of a righteous person has great power and produces wonderful results. My dear brothers and sisters, if someone among you wanders away from the truth and is brought back, you can be sure that whoever brings the sinner back from wandering will save that person from death and bring about the forgiveness of many sins.
3. Share with one another an area in which you've struggled or an area where you're currently struggling.

Warning: If you find you're stuck in an addictive pattern, there's hope. First, be honest before God and admit it. Talk to your discipler about getting help. Recovery takes time, one day at a time. It may be helpful to your recovery to first meet with a pastor for prayer and guidance. If you're facing an immediate crisis, contact a pastor at your church.

Interacting with Scripture

<u>Numbers 30:2 (NIV)</u> *When a man makes a vow to the Lord or takes an oath to obligate himself by a pledge, he must not break his word but must do everything he said.*

Notes:

<u>Malachi 2:14–15 (NIV)</u> *You ask, "Why?" It is because the Lord is the witness between you and the wife of your youth. You have been unfaithful to her, though she is your partner, the wife of your marriage covenant.*

Has not the one God made you? You belong to him in body and spirit. And what does the one God seek? Godly offspring. So be on your guard, and do not be unfaithful to the wife of your youth.

<u>Matthew 19:4–6 (NIV)</u> *"Haven't you read," he replied, "that at the beginning the Creator 'made them male and female,' and said, 'For this reason a man will leave his father and mother and be united to his wife, and the two will become one flesh'? So they are no longer two, but one. Therefore what God has joined together, let man not separate."*

<u>Hebrews 13:4 (NIV)</u> *Marriage should be honored by all, and the marriage bed kept pure, for God will judge the adulterer and all the sexually immoral.*

1. What stood out to you in the passages?
2. Why is sexual integrity essential as a follower of Christ, whether you're married or not?

A vow of faithfulness is the commitment to stay true to your marriage vows with fidelity and devotion, while a vow of chastity is the commitment to refrain from sex outside the covenant of marriage.

MARRIED

If you're married, renew your vow of faithfulness before God. If you can remember your marriage vows, create a sacred moment and renew those vows with your spouse.

Warning: If you have been or are being unfaithful to your spouse (emotionally, physically, or through pornography), first stop the behavior, confess before God your sin, repent, and rest in the forgiveness Christ offers. Then, confess your sin to your spouse and your discipler. Contact a pastor at your church to facilitate this process. Check thewayofdiscipleship.org for recommendations to help you move toward reconciliation.

SINGLE

If you aren't married, create a vow of chastity and share that with your discipler. If you're having sex outside of the marriage relationship or are engaging with pornography, first stop the behavior, confess your sin before God, repent, and rest in the forgiveness Christ offers. Then, confess your sin to your discipler. Contact a pastor at your church to help you move forward in freedom. 1 John 1:9 (NIV) *If we confess our sins, he is faithful and just and will forgive us our sins and purify us from all unrighteousness.*

 Breath Prayers are short prayers we utter frequently to refocus us on the constant presence of God.

Consider some of these breath prayers in times of temptation:
- "God, provide a way out." (based on 1 Corinthians 10:13)
- "Take this thought captive, Jesus." (based on 2 Corinthians 10:15)
- "I surrender all."
- "Lord, help me now!"

Growing in the Practice of Moral Integrity: At the beginning of this practice, you assessed where you were at that time. Now assess where you are today by answering these questions:

1. Where have I seen the most movement?
2. Where do I have the most room for growth?

 Discussion Prompts and Questions:

1. Review your responses to the Scriptures you've been reading. If you haven't read the Scripture prior to today, read it now and answer the questions together.
2. Discuss your thoughts regarding the spiritual disciplines of vows and breath prayers. Were these spiritual disciplines new to you?
3. What was the most difficult thing for you about these disciplines? How will you incorporate them into your life?
4. How does this practice relate to Surrender and Trust or Communion with God?

The Practice of Moral Integrity—Summary

Discuss before moving on to the next essential practice:

1. What have you learned about the Practice of Moral Integrity? Where have you seen the most movement? Where do you have the most room for growth?
2. How are you ensuring your actions aren't merely episodic, but that you're moving toward a lifestyle of moral integrity?
3. Now that you've experimented with some of the accompanying spiritual disciplines, circle the one on which you'll focus for the next thirty days, integrating it into your life:
   - **Studying the Bible**
   - **Journaling**
   - **Accountability**
   - **Vows of faithfulness or chastity**
   - **Breath prayers**

As a reminder, some spiritual disciplines will be more natural for you, while others will require intentional practice. Over time, you'll find a rhythm that's appropriate to your life stage and spiritual needs.

The Practice of Spiritual Community

What does it mean to live in community? How does this affect our ability to love, forgive and serve others? It means everything. We can only love, forgive, serve, bless, give, encourage, unite and have patience because we know who we are and where we live. We can do these things because Messiah Jesus has done them.

—J. B. Smith, The Good and Beautiful Community

Preparation for Your First Meeting

 ### Interacting with Scripture

<u>Psalm 133:1 (NIV)</u> *How good and pleasant it is when God's people live together in unity.*

<u>Acts 2:42–47 (NIV)</u> *They devoted themselves to the apostles' teaching and to fellowship, to the breaking of bread and to prayer. Everyone was filled with awe at the many wonders and signs performed by the apostles. All the believers were together and had everything in common. They sold property and possessions to give to anyone who had need. Every day they continued to meet together in the temple courts. They broke bread in their homes and ate together with glad and sincere hearts, praising God and enjoying the favor of all the people. And the Lord added to their number daily those who were being saved.*

 ### Practice Overview

Read through the following definition of the Practice of Spiritual Community. Highlight or underline the words or phrases that stand out to you.

Ordinary disciples of Jesus Christ are committed to living in spiritual communities through local churches.

Jesus disciples hunger for spiritual community—a gathering of fellow disciples; rich, spiritual friendships; and authentic mentoring relationships. They commit to and willingly submit to the authority of that community. Followers of Jesus know the power of authentic, redemptive relationships to encourage and strengthen one another, as well as to draw others to God. They believe "the Bible knows nothing of solitary religion" (John Wesley), and they believe it's a Christ follower's duty to engage others in authentic, redemptive relationships. Christ followers are open and responsive to the rebuke, correction, exhortation, and discipline of the church. Jesus' dream was for His followers to live in unity with one another, and He called them to love one another as He loved them.

Those who commit to these practices know the power of authentic, redemptive relationships. Their lives are shaped and guided by the example and encouragement of others in the faith, and they foster this community in others. When disciples live together in love, unity, and mutual support, their lives and the life of the church of Jesus Christ are strong and powerful in advancing God's kingdom in this world.

 Personal Assessment:

	Almost Never	Rarely	Occasionally	Frequently	Consistently	Not Sure
I experience the power of authentic, redemptive relationships in my life.	☐	☐	☐	☐	☐	☐
I'm shaped and guided by the example and encouragement of others in the faith.	☐	☐	☐	☐	☐	☐

	True	Not True	Not Sure
I live out spiritual community in my local church on a macro scale by participating with the broader church body in worship services and large-scale involvement.	☐	☐	☐
I live out spiritual community in my local church on a micro scale, specifically through engagement in a small group or ministry team.	☐	☐	☐

Discussion Prompts and Questions:

1. Based on the description and the Scripture you read, how would you describe spiritual community?

2. How have you experienced spiritual community? Share examples of what it's been like for you to practice this in your life.

3. Share your initial assessment on this practice.

4. What would need to change in order for you to intentionally increase the role of spiritual community in your life?

 Interacting with Scripture

1 Corinthians 12:14–27 (NIV) *Even so the body is not made up of one part but of many.*

Now if the foot should say, "Because I am not a hand, I do not belong to the body," it would not for that reason stop being part of the body. And if the ear should say, "Because I am not an eye, I do not belong to the body," it would not for that reason stop being part of the body. If the whole body were an eye, where would the sense of hearing be? If the whole body were an ear, where would the sense of smell be? But in fact God has placed the parts in the body, every one of them, just as he wanted them to be. If they were all one part, where would the body be? As it is, there are many parts, but one body.

The eye cannot say to the hand, "I don't need you!" And the head cannot say to the feet, "I don't need you!" On the contrary, those parts of the body that seem to be weaker are indispensable, and the parts that we think are less

Notes:

93

honorable we treat with special honor. And the parts that are unpresentable are treated with special modesty, while our presentable parts need no special treatment. But God has put the body together, giving greater honor to the parts that lacked it, so that there should be no division in the body, but that its parts should have equal concern for each other. If one part suffers, every part suffers with it; if one part is honored, every part rejoices with it.

Now you are the body of Christ, and each one of you is a part of it.

Notes:

1. What does this passage tell us about spiritual community?
2. Describe a time when you experienced a group of Christ followers working well together.
3. Pride, jealousy, and envy can cause division and strife among members of a community. How can we guard against these toxic traits?

 ## Spiritual Disciplines

Over the next few weeks, you'll try some disciplines integral in developing the Practice of Spiritual Community:

- **Corporate worship**
- **Corporate prayer**
- **Purposeful community**
- **Hospitality**
- **Submitting to a mentor**

True worship of God happens when we put God first in our lives. When what God says matters more than what others say, and when loving God matters more than being loved. Discipline, willpower, giftedness and going to church can be good things. But they do not guarantee transformation. Transformation comes through valuing God above all else. The heart of worship is to seek and to know God in our own unique way. Each one of us fulfills some part of the divine image. Each one of us loves and glorifies God in a particular way that no one else can.

—Calhoun, *Spiritual Disciplines Handbook*

 Corporate Worship: A corporate worship service is the approach a church takes in messaging the story and mission of God by creating congregational experiences at all age levels. Corporate worship helps people engage with God in ways that are transcendent and transformational by communicating the majesty, beauty, and goodness of God through words spoken, artistic expressions, music, rituals, and silent adoration.

The impact of a worship experience can be dramatically impacted by a few intentional efforts on your part. Rather than rushing into the weekend worship service, begin by creating margin prior to the service to allow you to be more fully present and attentive to God.

- Plan to arrive ten to fifteen minutes early. Take time to acknowledge others by pausing, making eye contact, and expressing warm spoken greetings.
- A few minutes before the service begins, sit quietly, noticing the sights and sounds surrounding you.
- Pray for those surrounding you. Ask God to minister to them.
- Assume a posture of expectation that God will meet you. Sit and/or stand with your hands open and palms up, ready to receive what God wants you to experience.
- Pay special attention to one element of worship each week.
- Focus on what God might be asking you to do. How might He be prompting you toward a new way of living? How might He be prompting the congregation toward a new way of living?

Corporate prayer is engaging in interactive conversation with God about what He and we are thinking, feeling, and doing together.

Preparation for Your Second Meeting

Serving others is a vital part of Spiritual Community. Take note of how Jesus exhibited the posture of servanthood in the following Scripture.

 Interacting with Scripture

<u>John 13:1–17 (NIV)</u> *It was just before the Passover Festival. Jesus knew that the hour had come for him to leave this world and go to the Father. Having loved his own who were in the world, he loved them to the end.*

The evening meal was in progress, and the devil had already prompted Judas, the son of Simon Iscariot, to betray Jesus. Jesus knew that the Father had put all things under his power, and that he had come from God and was returning to God; so he got up from the meal, took off his outer clothing, and wrapped a towel around his waist. After that, he poured water into a basin and began to wash his disciples' feet, drying them with the towel that was wrapped around him.

He came to Simon Peter, who said to him, "Lord, are you going to wash my feet?"

Jesus replied, "You do not realize now what I am doing, but later you will understand."

Notes:
_____

"No," said Peter, "you shall never wash my feet."

Jesus answered, "Unless I wash you, you have no part with me."

"Then, Lord," Simon Peter replied, "not just my feet but my hands and my head as well!"

Jesus answered, "Those who have had a bath need only to wash their feet; their whole body is clean. And you are clean, though not every one of you." For he knew who was going to betray him, and that was why he said not everyone was clean.

When he had finished washing their feet, he put on his clothes and returned to his place. "Do you understand what I have done for you?" he asked them. "You call me 'Teacher' and 'Lord,' and rightly so, for that is what I am. Now that I, your Lord and Teacher, have washed your feet, you also should wash one another's feet. I have set you an example that you should do as I have done for you. Very truly I tell you, no servant is greater than his master, nor is a messenger greater than the one who sent him. Now that you know these things, you will be blessed if you do them.

Notes:

1. What stood out to you in this passage?
2. How did Jesus' posture differ from what was expected in that time?
3. What would it look like for you to demonstrate a posture of humility and servanthood? Be specific.

Discussion Prompts and Questions:

1. Review your responses to the Scriptures you've been reading. If you haven't read the Scripture prior to today, read it now and answer the questions together.
2. Discuss your thoughts regarding corporate worship and prayer. What benefits do you see in approaching worship more intentionally? How can you adapt your approach to worship and prayer in order for it to be more meaningful?
3. What are you learning about the important aspects of spiritual community from the Scripture and the disciplines of corporate worship and prayer?

Preparation for Your Third Meeting

 ## Interacting with Scripture

1 Corinthians 11:17–34 (NIV) *In the following directives I have no praise for you, for your meetings do more harm than good. In the first place, I hear that when you come together as a church, there are divisions among you, and to some extent I believe it. No doubt there have to be differences among you to show which of you have God's approval. So then, when you come together, it is not the Lord's Supper you eat, for when you are eating, some of you go ahead with your own private suppers. As a result, one person remains hungry and another gets drunk. Don't you have homes to eat and drink in? Or do you despise the church of God by humiliating those who have nothing? What shall I say to you? Shall I praise you? Certainly not in this matter!*

For I received from the Lord what I also passed on to you: The Lord Jesus, on the night he was betrayed, took bread, and when he had given thanks, he broke it and said, "This is my body, which is for you; do this in

Notes:

remembrance of me." In the same way, after supper he took the cup, saying, "This cup is the new covenant in my blood; do this, whenever you drink it, in remembrance of me." For whenever you eat this bread and drink this cup, you proclaim the Lord's death until he comes.

So then, whoever eats the bread or drinks the cup of the Lord in an unworthy manner will be guilty of sinning against the body and blood of the Lord. Everyone ought to examine themselves before they eat of the bread and drink from the cup. For those who eat and drink without discerning the body of Christ eat and drink judgment on themselves. That is why many among you are weak and sick, and a number of you have fallen asleep. But if we were more discerning with regard to ourselves, we would not come under such judgment. Nevertheless, when we are judged in this way by the Lord, we are being disciplined so that we will not be finally condemned with the world.

So then, my brothers and sisters, when you gather to eat, you should all eat together. Anyone who is hungry should eat something at home, so that when you meet together it may not result in judgment. And when I come I will give further directions.

Matthew 18:15–20 (NIV) *If your brother or sister sins, go and point out their fault, just between the two of you. If they listen to you, you have won them over. But if they will not listen, take one or two others along, so that "every matter may be established by the testimony of two or three witnesses." If they still refuse to listen, tell it to the church; and if they refuse to listen even to the church, treat them as you would a pagan or a tax collector.*

Notes:

Truly I tell you, whatever you bind on earth will be bound in heaven, and whatever you loose on earth will be loosed in heaven.

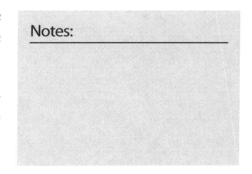

Notes:

Again, truly I tell you that if two of you on earth agree about anything they ask for, it will be done for them by my Father in heaven. For where two or three gather in my name, there am I with them.

1. What stood out to you in these passages?
2. What can you learn from these passages about Biblically dealing with difficulties and conflicts?
3. Spiritual community includes committing to and actually living alongside others. List some of the many benefits of living in spiritual community. What's most difficult for you when it comes to being part of a spiritual community?

 Hospitality is inviting others into our homes and lives, to build relationships and natural opportunities to share our lives and faith.

 Purposeful community is intentionally sharing life with a small group of people for study, prayer, care, and accountability.

 Submitting to a mentor is the process of meeting with a trusted individual for particular guidance in an area of your spiritual life.

These disciplines invite us to open our lives to others in increasing measures. Peter speaks to the critical nature of community in the following verses.

Interacting with Scripture

<u>1 Peter 4:7–11 (NIV)</u> *The end of all things is near. Therefore be alert and of sober mind so that you may pray. Above all, love each other deeply, because love covers over a multitude of sins. Offer hospitality to one another without grumbling. Each of you should use whatever gift you have received to serve others, as faithful stewards of God's grace in its various forms. If anyone speaks, they should do so as one who speaks the very words of God. If anyone serves, they should do so with the strength God provides, so that in all things God may be praised through Jesus Christ. To him be the glory and the power for ever and ever. Amen.*

Notes:

1. What stood out to you in Peter's words?
2. How have you participated in spiritual community, specifically in...

	Past	Present
offering hospitality?		
purposeful community?		
submitting to a mentor?		

3. What's hindering you from participating in these disciplines?
4. What can you do to grow in one or all of these areas?

Growing in the Practice of Spiritual Community: At the beginning of this practice you assessed where you were at that time. Now assess where you are today.

1. Where have I seen the most movement?
2. Where do I have the most room for growth?

 Discussion Prompts and Questions:

1. Review your responses to the Scriptures you've been reading. If you haven't read the Scripture prior to today, read it now and answer the questions together.
2. Discuss your thoughts regarding the spiritual disciplines of purposeful small-group community and hospitality.
3. What was the most difficult thing for you about these disciplines? How will you incorporate them into your life?

The Practice of Spiritual Community—Summary

Discuss before moving on to the next essential practice:

What have you learned about the Practice of Spiritual Community? Where have you seen the most movement? Where do you have the most room for growth?

Participating in spiritual community requires you to willingly commit and submit to the authority of that community. Living in authentic, redemptive relationships means we agree to be open and responsive to the correction and exhortation of others.

What's your next step to be connected and committed your church community?

Read the following Scripture, pausing to realize the significant role we as ordinary disciples of Jesus Christ are called to play in our world.

Interacting with Scripture

<u>Romans 12:4–18 (NIV)</u> *Just as each of us has one body with many members, and these members do not all have the same function so in Christ we who are many form one body, and each member belongs to all the others. We have different gifts, according to the grace given us. If a man's gift is prophesying, let him use it in proportion to his faith. If it is serving, let him serve; if it is teaching, let him teach; if it is encouraging, let him encourage; if it is contributing to the needs of others, let him give generously; if it is leadership, let him govern diligently; if it is showing mercy, let him do it cheerfully.*

Love must be sincere. Hate what is evil; cling to what is good. Be devoted to one another in brotherly love. Honor one another above yourselves. Never be lacking in zeal, but keep your spiritual fervor, serving the Lord. Be joyful in hope, patient in affliction, faithful in prayer. Share with God's people who are in need. Practice hospitality. Bless those who persecute you; bless and do not curse. Rejoice with those who rejoice; mourn with those who mourn. Live in harmony with one another. Do not be proud, but be willing to associate with people of low position. Do not be conceited. Do not repay anyone evil for evil. Be careful to do what is right in the eyes of everybody. If it is possible, as far as it depends on you, live at peace with everyone.

Notes: _____

Close your time on this practice by thanking God for including you in His plan to change the world. Commit to standing alongside others in community and advancing God's kingdom in this world!

Practices That Branch Out and Bear Fruit

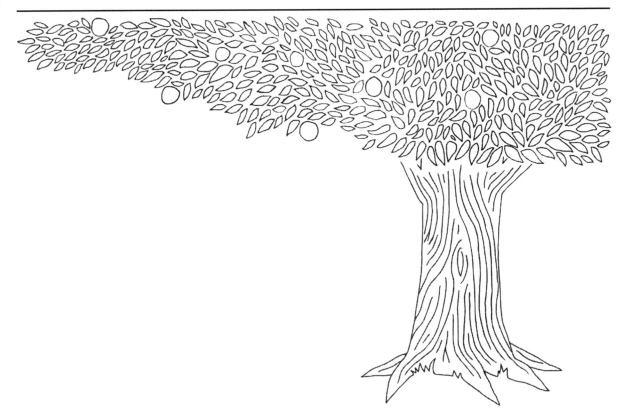

The Practice of Seeking the Call of God

> Modern life assaults us with an infinite range of things we could do, we would love to do, or some people tell us we should do. But we are not God and we are neither infinite nor eternal. We are quite simply finite. We have only so many years, so much energy, so many gray cells, and so many bank notes in our wallets. "Life is too short to..." eventually shortens to, "Life is too short."
>
> —Guinness, The Call

Preparation for Your First Meeting

Prepare to engage in the Practice of Seeking the Call of God by focusing on this core truth: you are God's masterpiece, made for His purposes.

 ## Interacting with Scripture

Read Ephesians 2:10 and commit this verse to memory over the next few weeks:

Ephesians 2:10 (NLT) *For we are God's masterpiece. He has created us anew in Christ Jesus, so we can do the good things he planned for us long ago.*

 ## Practice Overview

Read through the following definition of the Practice of Seeking the Call of God. Highlight or underline the words or phrases that stand out to you.

Ordinary disciples of Jesus Christ seek the call of God on their lives.

God created His followers with unique purposes and destinies. Each one has been called to tell God's story and build His kingdom through that disciple's gifts, abilities, and life circumstances. As disciples of Jesus, God's followers must discover and engage their unique callings—whether it means leading people to redemption in Christ, engaging in issues of justice and mercy, providing loving community, or bringing healing and reconciliation. It's up to every disciple of Jesus to move beyond careers, roles, and job titles to discover the callings God has had in mind for him or her since before he or she was even born.

As Jesus' followers live out their callings and mission, with the help of the Holy Spirit, their unique gifts meet the world's unique needs. As a result, they experience a deeper sense of meaning and fulfillment—and the world experiences a deeper change for the good.

 Personal Assessment:

	Strongly Disagree	Somewhat Disagree	Somewhat Agree	Strongly Agree
I know God created me as a masterpiece for His purposes.	☐	☐	☐	☐
I understand that calling is a process of listening and responding to God.	☐	☐	☐	☐
I live with a God-given purpose beyond my career, role, or job title.	☐	☐	☐	☐
I experience a deep sense of meaning and fulfillment in my life.	☐	☐	☐	☐

1. Have you ever considered that God desires to tell His story and build His kingdom through your gifts, abilities, and life circumstances? Is this a new idea for you to consider?
2. How does it make you feel to consider that God created you as His masterpiece for His purposes?

Lifeline

Part of seeking the call of God is to see how God's already been involved in your life. In preparation for your first meeting, complete the following lifeline.

1. Starting at birth, plot five- to ten-year increments on the scale, based on your age.
2. Moving from left to right, list significant people or events that have influenced who you are today. Be sure to include both highs (on top) and lows (below).

(+) **Highs** (dreams, interests, positive experiences, and influential people)

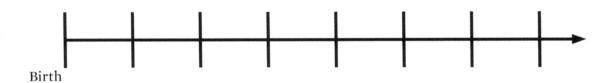

Birth

(-) **Lows** (losses, hurts, disappointments, difficult experiences and negative influences)

1. Review your lifeline. List out below the three most significant people or events:
2. What themes, if any, do you see flowing through your lifeline?
3. How did these events or people shape your understanding of who God is? How did your perspective of God change throughout the years?

 ### Discussion Prompts and Questions:

1. If someone were to ask you to describe what it means to seek the call of God, what would you say?
2. Share your initial assessment on this practice.
3. Take turns sharing your lifelines with one another, making sure to mention the three most significant people or events you listed. As each of you shares, ask the Holy Spirit to guide you to whatever God wants you to notice.
   - Did this exercise help you become more aware of God's activity in your life?
   - Are you noticing any themes in your lifeline?
   - Take some time after each of you shares to pray for one another.

Preparation for Your Second Meeting

God's been calling His people to His purposes since the beginning. Read the following Old Testament stories, taking note of what you observe related to seeking the call of God.

 ## Interacting with Scripture

Isaiah 6:1–8 (NIV) *In the year that King Uzziah died, I saw the Lord, high and exalted, seated on a throne; and the train of his robe filled the temple. Above him were seraphim, each with six wings: With two wings they covered their faces, with two they covered their feet, and with two they were flying. And they were calling to one another:*

"Holy, holy, holy is the Lord Almighty;
the whole earth is full of his glory."

At the sound of their voices the doorposts and thresholds shook and the temple was filled with smoke. "Woe to me!" I cried. "I am ruined! For I am a man of unclean lips, and I live among a people of unclean lips, and my eyes have seen the King, the Lord Almighty."

Then one of the seraphim flew to me with a live coal in his hand, which he had taken with tongs from the altar. With it he touched my mouth and said, "See, this has touched your lips; your guilt is taken away and your sin atoned for." Then I heard the voice of the Lord saying, "Whom shall I send? And who will go for us?" And I said, "Here am I. Send me!"

Notes:

<u>Esther 4:12–14 (NIV)</u> *When Esther's words were reported to Mordecai, he sent back this answer: "Do not think that because you are in the king's house you alone of all the Jews will escape. For if you remain silent at this time, relief and deliverance for the Jews will arise from another place, but you and your father's family will perish. And who knows but that you have come to your royal position for such a time as this?"*

Notes:

1. What do these passages suggest about calling?
2. How do you relate to Isaiah's circumstance? To Esther's?
3. Look back over your lifeline. Describe a situation when you sensed God used you for "such a time as this."

 Spiritual Disciplines Over the next few weeks, you'll try some disciplines integral in developing the Practice of Seeking the Call of God:

- **Contemplative prayer**
- **Meditative prayer**
- **Investigating your spiritual gifts**
- **Submitting to a mentor**
- **Serving others**

Seeking the call of God isn't a one-time event but a dynamic process of listening to God and responding to what He says. Certain spiritual disciplines, such as contemplative prayer and meditative prayer, will help cultivate listening.

God made you to flourish, but flourishing never happens by looking out for "number one." It is tied to a grander and nobler vision. The world badly needs wise and flourishing human beings, and we are called to bring God's glory to the world.

—Ortberg, *The Me I Want to Be*

The Practice of Seeking the Call of God also entails connecting the dots between God's purposes and how He's made you. You are God's masterpiece, uniquely created with particular spiritual gifts, abilities, and a unique temperament for the accomplishment of His purposes, or mission.

We understand the Mission of God as restoring broken places in the world. In the next several weeks, you'll be experimenting with various spiritual disciplines and related assessments to help you discover God's call on your life to restore at least one of those broken places. As a disciple, you'll experiment with the discipline of submitting to a mentor as well as the discipline of service in order to step more fully into your calling.

 Contemplative prayer is prayer without words to cultivate attentiveness and listening to God.

Try this discipline between now and when you meet next with your discipler. Take the first and last five minutes of your day in contemplative prayer.

1. As soon as you wake up, pause for five minutes in silence and use this as your prayer today: "Yes, God." Meditate on what it would be like to say, "Yes, God," when He speaks. Throughout the day, practice saying, "Yes, God," to what He shows you or asks you to do.
2. At the end of each day, also pause for five minutes. Reflect on your day. What did you notice in saying and practicing, "Yes, God"?
3. If you're journaling, keep a daily log of your prayer and practice of, "Yes, God."

 Discussion Prompts and Questions:

1. Review your responses to the Scriptures you've been reading. If you haven't read the Scripture prior to today, read it now and answer the questions together.
2. How has your daily contemplative prayer practice impacted the way you see? What have you been noticing in praying and in practicing, "Yes, God"? Note in this simple practice that we can daily respond to the call of God by saying, "Yes," to Him.

Preparation for Your Third Meeting

 Interacting with Scripture

<u>Psalm 139 (NIV)</u> *You have searched me, L*ORD,
and you know me.
You know when I sit and when I rise;
you perceive my thoughts from afar.
You discern my going out and my lying down;
you are familiar with all my ways.
Before a word is on my tongue
*you, L*ORD*, know it completely.*
You hem me in behind and before,
and you lay your hand upon me.
Such knowledge is too wonderful for me,
too lofty for me to attain.

Where can I go from your Spirit?
Where can I flee from your presence?

If I go up to the heavens, you are there;
if I make my bed in the depths, you are there.
If I rise on the wings of the dawn,
if I settle on the far side of the sea,
even there your hand will guide me,
your right hand will hold me fast.
If I say, "Surely the darkness will hide me
and the light become night around me,"
even the darkness will not be dark to you;
the night will shine like the day,
for darkness is as light to you.

For you created my inmost being;
you knit me together in my mother's womb.
I praise you because I am fearfully and wonderfully made;

Notes:

your works are wonderful,
I know that full well.
My frame was not hidden from you
when I was made in the secret place,
when I was woven together in the depths of the earth.
Your eyes saw my unformed body;
all the days ordained for me were written in your book
before one of them came to be.
How precious to me are your thoughts, God!
How vast is the sum of them!
Were I to count them,
they would outnumber the grains of sand—
when I awake, I am still with you.
If only you, God, would slay the wicked!
Away from me, you who are bloodthirsty!
They speak of you with evil intent;
your adversaries misuse your name.
Do I not hate those who hate you, Lord,
and abhor those who are in rebellion against you?
I have nothing but hatred for them;
I count them my enemies.
Search me, God, and know my heart;
test me and know my anxious thoughts.
See if there is any offensive way in me,
and lead me in the way everlasting.

Notes:

1. What stood out to you in the passage?
2. What do you notice about God from this passage? What did you notice about yourself?
3. How does this passage speak to the contrast between the vast nature of God and the particular nature of God in how He formed you and me?

Meditative prayer is focused concentration and reflection on something God's said through Scripture.

1. Every day this week, take a few moments to read and reflect on Psalm 139:13–14. Consider memorizing this verse.

    Psalm 139:13–14 (NIV) *For you created my inmost being; you knit me together in my mother's womb. I praise you because I am fearfully and wonderfully made; your works are wonderful, I know that full well.*

2. As you reflect on this passage, ask God to show you one thing to which He wants you to pay attention.

 Discussion Prompts and Questions:

1. Review your responses to the Scriptures you've been reading. If you haven't read the Scripture prior to today, read it now and discuss your experience with meditative prayer.

2. How has your experience with meditative prayer—focused on Psalm 139:13–14— impacted how you see God? How you see yourself?

One of the most incredible realities of following Christ is that God Himself invites us to be part of fulfilling His purposes. Ephesians 1:8–10 (NIV) *With all wisdom and understanding, he made known to us the mystery of his will according to his good pleasure, which he purposed in Christ, to be put into effect when the times reach their fulfillment—to bring unity to all things in heaven and on earth under Christ.*

The place God calls you to is the place where your deep gladness and the world's deep hunger meet.
—Buechner *Wishful Thinking*

The Six Broken Places

At Grace Church, we define the mission of God as restoring Six Broken Places in the world, which are a result of the fall of humanity and ongoing disobedience against God. This brief assessment will help you determine: which of these six places troubles you the most, the places God is already using you, and what God could be calling you to. It's likely that whichever troubles you the most or the place God's already using you could be related to a specific call God has for you.

Take a moment together to read through the following list of the Six Broken Places. Check three of these that trouble you most.

The Six Broken Places in the World	Check the three that trouble you most.
SEPARATION: Human beings are alienated from God and lost.	
PAIN: Human beings' bodies, minds, and spirits are broken.	
ISOLATION: Human beings are alone and lack loving relationships.	
HATRED: Human beings alienate and dehumanize each other, resulting in discrimination, racism, war, and genocide.	
DECAY: The physical creation is deteriorating and "groaning" because of abuse and neglect by human beings.	
INJUSTICE: Injustice abounds everywhere, resulting in systems of poverty, hunger, disease, and slavery, among others.	

1. Circle the one broken place that *most* troubles you.
2. Finish the following statements:
   - "I'm most troubled by this because..."
   - "God, if I could do anything to help heal this broken place, it would be..."

Interacting with Scripture

Notes:

<u>Ephesians 2:6–10 (NIV)</u> *And God raised us up with Christ and seated us with him in the heavenly realms in Christ Jesus, in order that in the coming ages he might show the incomparable riches of his grace, expressed in his kindness to us in Christ Jesus. For it is by grace you have been saved, through faith—and this is not from yourselves, it is the gift of God—not by works, so that no one can boast. For we are God's handiwork, created in Christ Jesus to do good works, which God prepared in advance for us to do.*

<u>Psalm 40:4–6 (NIV)</u> *Blessed is the one who trusts in the Lord, who does not look to the proud, to those who turn aside to false gods. Many, Lord my God, are the wonders you have done, the things you planned for us. None can compare with you; were I to speak and tell of your deeds, they would be too many to declare. Sacrifice and offering you did not desire –but my ears you have opened—burnt offerings and sin offerings you did not require.*

1. According to these passages what do you think about God's purposes?
2. What do you believe is our part in fulfilling His purposes?

Likely, God is already using you to heal a broken place in this world. Start with the one that troubles you most. Answer the questions about each broken place in the space provided.

The Six Broken Places in the World		How has God already been using you? Write down specific people, places, events, etc.
	SEPARATION: Human beings are alienated from God and lost.	
	PAIN: Human beings' bodies, minds, and spirits are broken.	
	ISOLATION: Human beings are alone and lack loving relationships.	
	HATRED: Human beings alienate and dehumanize each other, resulting in discrimination, racism, war, and genocide.	
	DECAY: The physical creation is deteriorating and "groaning" because of abuse and neglect by human beings.	
	INJUSTICE: Injustice abounds everywhere, resulting in systems of poverty, hunger, disease, and slavery, among others.	

Preparation for Your Fourth Meeting

 Interacting with Scripture

Ephesians 4:1–14 (NLT) *Therefore I, a prisoner for serving the Lord, beg you to lead a life worthy of your calling, for you have been called by God. Be humble and gentle. Be patient with each other,*

making allowance for each other's faults because of your love. Always keep yourselves united in the Holy Spirit, and bind yourselves together with peace.

We are all one body, we have the same Spirit, and we have all been called to the same glorious future. There is only one Lord, one faith, one baptism, and there is only one God and Father, who is over us all and in us all and living through us all. However, he has given each one of us a special gift according to the generosity of Christ. That is why the Scriptures say,

"When he ascended to the heights,
he led a crowd of captives
and gave gifts to his people."

Notice that it says "he ascended." This means that Christ first came down to the lowly world in which we live. The same one who came down is the one who ascended higher than all the heavens, so that his rule might fill the entire universe.

He is the one who gave these gifts to the church: the apostles, the prophets, the evangelists, and the pastors and teachers. Their responsibility is to equip God's people to do his work and build up the church, the body of Christ, until we come to such unity in our faith and knowledge of God's Son that we will be mature and full grown in the Lord, measuring up to the full stature of Christ.

Then we will no longer be immature like children. We won't be tossed and blown about by every wind of new teaching. We will not be influenced when people try to trick us with lies so clever they sound like truth.

Notes:

2 Timothy 1:6–7 (NIV) For this reason I remind you to fan into flame the gift of God, which is in you through the laying on of my hands. For the Spirit God gave us does not make us timid, but gives us power, love and self-discipline.

Romans 12:3–8 (NIV) For by the grace given me I say to every one of you: Do not think of yourself more highly than you ought, but rather think of yourself with sober judgment, in accordance with the faith God has distributed to each of you. For just as each of us has one body with many members, and these members do not all have the same function, so in Christ we, though many, form one body, and each member belongs to all the others. We have different gifts, according to the grace given to each of us. If your gift is prophesying, then prophesy in accordance with your faith; if it is serving, then serve; if it is teaching, then teach; if it is to encourage, then give encouragement; if it is giving, then give generously; if it is to lead, do it diligently; if it is to show mercy, do it cheerfully.

Notes:

1. According to Ephesians 4, what do you notice in terms of the purpose and provision of gifts? Where do they come from, and why do we have them?
2. From 2 Timothy 1:6–7, what does the Spirit of God give us as we seek the call of God and begin using our gifts?
3. Spiritual gifts aren't to be viewed from an individualistic perspective but from a communal perspective of glorifying God and benefiting others. How might some of the gifts mentioned in Romans 12 benefit others and glorify God?

Investigating your spiritual gifts is the process of learning your unique spiritual gift mix to help you discover what God is calling you to do in service to Him and others.

If you haven't had the opportunity to discover your spiritual gifting, spend about fifteen minutes completing this free spiritual gifts assessment at ministrymatters.com/spiritualgifts. Print out your results.

Gaining the perspective of others who know you well concerning your spiritual gifts can be very insightful. List your top three spiritual gifts below. Then, ask two people who know you well to share what spiritual gifts they've seen in you. Write their answers below to see how they contrast with those indicated on your assessment:

What did the assessment show are my top three spiritual gifts?	From another's perspective, what are my top three spiritual gifts?	From another's perspective, what are my top three spiritual gifts?
1.	1.	1.
2.	2.	2.
3.	3.	3.

(OPTIONAL) In addition to your spiritual gifts, you have a unique strength, personality, and learning style. Several free assessments are available online if you need help in assessing the ways God has uniquely created you. For more information, go to thewayofdiscipleship.org.

Growing in the Practice of Seeking the Call of God: At the beginning of this practice you assessed where you were at that time. Now assess where you are today.

1. Where have I seen the most movement?
2. Where do I have the most room for growth?

 Discussion Prompts and Questions:

1. Review your responses to the Scriptures you've been reading. If you haven't read the Scripture prior to today, read it now and answer the questions together.
2. Review the results from your assessments.
   a. What have you learned about yourself?
   b. How could these insights impact where and how you use your gifts and serve God in His work?
3. Review your responses to the Six Broken Places assessment and related questions.

 Submitting to a mentor is the process of meeting with a trusted individual for particular guidance in an area of your spiritual life.

By the very nature of The Way of Discipleship, you're already experiencing this dynamic at a certain level. When you seek another person's guidance, you expand your perspectives and ability to discern God's calling as he or she reflects back to you what he or she sees in you.

Over the next few months, commit to finding a person you can mentor. Here are some steps to finding a person to mentor:

1. Begin by looking at the various people God's placed in your life.
2. Consider what you have that you might want to share with someone else. For example, if you're gifted in prayer, become a prayer partner with a younger person. If you're in an older, established marriage, mentor a newly married couple and share your life with them. If you're established in your chosen vocation, mentor a person just entering his

or her career. If you're in high school and remembering navigating the difficult early-adolescent years, mentor a younger student by offering him or her a listening ear and encouraging word.

3. Set up a time to meet or talk with this person and let him or her know you're willing and open to getting to know one another more and walking together as he or she grows. Commit to a specified time period between meetings. Review with your mentee some of the work you've done over these weeks with the Way of the Discipleship.

Connecting the dots between your abilities (strengths) and spiritual gifts may help you discover how you could contribute to helping restore at least one of the Six Broken Places. Take some time to review your responses to this section, paying attention to which of the Six Broken Places troubles you the most and how you've been uniquely created to tell God's story and build His kingdom.

 Serving others is using one's unique passions, abilities, and spiritual gifts as a way to love God and love others.

As we serve, we discover what we enjoy doing, we understand better our passions, and we see our spiritual gifts in action.

1. What action step can I take now to move toward bringing healing in one or more of the Six Broken Places?
2. What's my next step? (Who can I contact? What can I read? Where can I serve?)

The Practice of Seeking the Call of God—Summary

Discuss before moving on to the next essential practice:

1. What have you learned about the Practice of Seeking the Call of God? Where have you seen the most movement? Where do you have the most room for growth?
2. Where have you seen personal growth? What needs to change in your life in order for you continue to grow in the Practice of Seeking the Call of God?

3. Now that you've experimented with some of the accompanying spiritual disciplines, focus on at least one of these disciplines going forward:

- **Contemplative prayer**
- **Meditative prayer**
- **Investigating your spiritual gifts**
- **Submitting to a mentor**
- **Serving others**

As a reminder, some spiritual disciplines will be more natural for you, while others will require intentional practice. Over time, you'll find a rhythm that's appropriate to your life stage and spiritual needs.

The Practice of Justice and Mercy

The gospel means much more than the personal salvation of individuals. It means a social revolution.

—Stearns, The Hole in Our Gospel

Preparation for Your First Meeting

Prepare to engage in the Practice of Justice and Mercy by reading each passage below a few times. Choose one to commit to memory over the next few weeks.

<u>Isaiah 58:10 (NIV)</u> *If you spend yourselves in behalf of the hungry and satisfy the needs of the oppressed, then your light will rise in the darkness, and your night will become like the noonday.*

<u>Luke 4:18–19 (NIV)</u> *The Spirit of the Lord is on me, because he has anointed me to proclaim good news to the poor. He has sent me to proclaim freedom for the prisoners and recovery of sight for the blind, to set the oppressed free, to proclaim the year of the Lord's favor.*

 Practice Overview

Read through the following definition of the Practice of Justice and Mercy. Highlight or underline the words or phrases that stand out to you.

Ordinary disciples of Jesus Christ engage in lifestyles of Justice and Mercy.

Every day we hear of indescribable injustices around the world. Disciples of Jesus aren't only aware of them, but they're also engaged in the mission to confront them. These injustices include the crushing cycle of poverty, the scourge of debilitating illnesses, the constant hatred and hostilities among peoples, the destruction of the physical creation, and the evil of human trafficking, among many others. Ordinary followers of Jesus passionately and actively seek to know their roles in addressing these injustices with selfless hearts motivated by love and service.

When disciples of Jesus engage the world of injustice, things happen. Followers of Christ, through the power of the Holy Spirit, develop compassion and a sense of spiritual authority that courageously confronts the evil systems of injustice. They have the joy of being Jesus in the eyes of the "least of these." As they become more aware of who God is and who they are, they have the thrill of being on "the borderland of the supernatural" where God is actively at work and the enemy is pushing back hard. On occasion, things actually change—people are delivered of spiritual bondage, a child is healed, a woman is rescued, a young man escapes the cycle of poverty, and God's kingdom agenda is furthered to His glory.

 Personal Assessment:

When I see the poor and marginalized, I have a tendency to judge them.	Strongly Disagree ☐	Somewhat Disagree ☐	Somewhat Agree ☐	Strongly Agree ☐		
I know the name of a person who's poor or marginalized.	Strongly Disagree ☐	Somewhat Disagree ☐	Somewhat Agree ☐	Strongly Agree ☐		
I know my role in confronting injustice in this world.	Strongly Disagree ☐	Somewhat Disagree ☐	Somewhat Agree ☐	Strongly Agree ☐		

I'm addressing injustice through love and service on a regular basis.	Almost Never ☐	Rarely ☐	Occasionally ☐	Frequently ☐	Consistently ☐	Not Sure ☐

Discussion Prompts and Questions:

1. If someone were to ask you to describe what the Practice of Justice and Mercy means, what would you say?
2. Give examples of what it's been like for you to practice Justice and Mercy throughout your life.
3. Share your initial assessment on this practice.
4. What ways do you see God currently leading you to actively engage in acts of Justice and Mercy?

Many passages in Scripture speak to justice and mercy. Read the following passages together, taking note of what you observe.

Interacting with Scripture

Deuteronomy 15:7–11 (NIV) *If anyone is poor among your fellow Israelites in any of the towns of the land the Lord your God is giving you, do not be hardhearted or tightfisted toward them. Rather, be openhanded and freely lend them whatever they need. Be careful not to harbor this wicked thought: "The seventh year, the year for canceling debts, is near," so that you do not show ill will toward the needy among your fellow Israelites and give them nothing. They may then appeal to the Lord against you, and you will be found guilty of sin. Give generously to them and do so without a grudging heart; then because of this the Lord your God will bless you in all your work and in everything you put your hand to. There will always be poor people in the land. Therefore I command you to be openhanded toward your fellow Israelites who are poor and needy in your land.*

Notes:

Matthew 25:31–46 (NIV) *When the Son of Man comes in his glory, and all the angels with him, he will sit on his glorious throne. All the nations will be gathered before him, and he will separate the people one from another as a shepherd separates the sheep from the goats. He will put the sheep on his right and the goats on his left.*

Then the King will say to those on his right, "Come, you who are blessed by my Father; take your inheritance, the kingdom prepared for you since the creation of the world. For I was hungry and you gave me something to eat, I was thirsty and you gave me something to drink, I was a stranger and you invited me in, I needed clothes and you clothed me, I was sick and you looked after me, I was in prison and you came to visit me." Then the righteous will answer him, "Lord, when did we see you hungry and feed you, or thirsty and give you something to drink? When did we see you a stranger and invite you in, or needing clothes and clothe you? When did we see you sick or in prison and go to visit you?"

The King will reply, "Truly I tell you, whatever you did for one of the least of these brothers and sisters of mine, you did for me."

Then he will say to those on his left, "Depart from me, you who are cursed, into the eternal fire prepared for the devil and his angels. For I was hungry and you gave me nothing to eat, I was thirsty and you gave me nothing to drink, I was a stranger and you did not invite me in, I needed clothes and you did not clothe me, I was sick and in prison and you did not look after me."

They also will answer, "Lord, when did we see you hungry or thirsty or a stranger or needing clothes or sick or in prison, and did not help you?"

Notes:

He will reply, "Truly I tell you, whatever you did not do for one of the least of these, you did not do for me." Then they will go away to eternal punishment, but the righteous to eternal life.

<u>Psalm 146:6–9 (NIV)</u>
He is the Maker of heaven and earth,
the sea, and everything in them—
he remains faithful forever.

He upholds the cause of the oppressed
and gives food to the hungry.

The Lord sets prisoners free,
the Lord gives sight to the blind,
the Lord lifts up those who are bowed down,
the Lord loves the righteous.

The Lord watches over the foreigner
and sustains the fatherless and the widow,
but he frustrates the ways of the wicked.

Notes:

1. What do these passages tell us about justice and mercy?
2. How much does your own heart reflect God's heart for the poor, oppressed, and marginalized?

 ## Spiritual Disciplines

Over the next few weeks, you'll try two disciplines integral in developing the Practice of Justice and Mercy:

- **Serving the poor and marginalized**
- **Peacemaking**

We define justice as simply acting right in our relationships, as determining how we stand in relation to others in our world.

—Samson, *Justice in the Burbs*

 Serving the poor and marginalized is the process of releasing one's own agenda and need for accomplishment and humbly submitting oneself to be in the presence of the poor and marginalized.

This discipline offers time, compassion, and resources for those who are stuck in the cycle of poverty or who live on the margins of society. At Grace Church, we prefer that serving is done in the context of long-term, authentic relationships, such as with trusted partners, thus minimizing exploitation of the poor.

NOTE: Read ahead for an understanding of what will be required of your second meeting. We recommend that you either participate in a short-term experience with a local outreach opportunity or plan over the next few months to take a short-term mission trip.

Preparation for Your Second Meeting

 Interacting with Scripture

Luke 10: 25–37(NIV) *On one occasion an expert in the law stood up to test Jesus. "Teacher," he asked, "what must I do to inherit eternal life?"*

"What is written in the Law?" he replied. "How do you read it?"

He answered, "Love the Lord your God with all your heart and with all your soul and with all your strength and with all your mind; and, Love your neighbor as yourself."

Notes:

"You have answered correctly," Jesus replied. "Do this and you will live."

But he wanted to justify himself, so he asked Jesus, "And who is my neighbor?"

In reply Jesus said: "A man was going down from Jerusalem to Jericho, when he was attacked by robbers. They stripped him of his clothes, beat him and went away, leaving him half dead. A priest happened to be going down the same road, and when he saw the man, he passed by on the other side. So too, a Levite, when he came to the place and saw him, passed by on the other side. But a Samaritan, as he traveled, came where the man was; and when he saw him, he took pity on him. He went to him and bandaged his wounds, pouring on oil and wine. Then he put the man on his own donkey, brought him to an inn and took care of him. The next day he took out two denarii and gave them to the innkeeper. 'Look after him,' he said, 'and when I return, I will reimburse you for any extra expense you may have.'"

Notes:

"Which of these three do you think was a neighbor to the man who fell into the hands of robbers?" The expert in the law replied, "The one who had mercy on him." Jesus told him, "Go and do likewise."

1. What stood out to you in the passage?
2. Who do you most identify with in the passage and why?
3. What attitude will you have when you serve this week? Pray that God will reveal Himself to you during your experience serving.

Serve together with a local outreach opportunity through your church or community. After serving together, discuss the following:

1. What were some of the feelings you had throughout your serving engagement?
2. Where did you see God?
3. What did God reveal to you about yourself?
4. What are you learning about living a life marked by justice and mercy?

Preparation for Your Third Meeting

 Interacting with Scripture

Proverbs 31:8–9 (NIV) *Speak up for those who cannot speak for themselves, for the rights of all who are destitute. Speak up and judge fairly; defend the rights of the poor and needy.*

Romans 12:15–18 (NIV) *Rejoice with those who rejoice; mourn with those who mourn. Live in harmony with one another. Do not be proud, but be willing to associate with people of low position. Do not be conceited. Do not repay anyone evil for evil. Be careful to do what is right in the eyes of everyone. If it is possible, as far as it depends on you, live at peace with everyone.*

Zechariah 7:9–10 (NIV) *This is what the Lord Almighty said: 'Administer true justice; show mercy and compassion to one another. Do not oppress the widow or the fatherless, the foreigner or the poor. Do not plot evil against each other.'*

Notes:

1. What stood out to you in these passages?
2. How can your voice be heard?
3. How could your gifts be used on behalf of the poor and marginalized?

 Peacemaking is the process of encouraging constructive resolution of conflict between individuals, people groups, races, or countries. It also might include the pursuit of racial reconciliation.

In order to see peacemaking integrated into our lives, we first have to confront our own perspectives, rooted in our family systems and cultural norms. Reread the peacemaking statement and answer the questions below:

1. Was peacemaking, even racial reconciliation, modeled in your home? If yes, what did you see modeled well? If not, how do you think that has impacted your current perspective?
2. Think back to your serving experience. What differences did you notice between those serving and those being served? What similarities?

To make peacemaking a part of our lives, we must move beyond just *serving* those who are different from us. We need to build trusting relationships. Examine your relationships. Do you have any relationships outside your race, people group, or nationality? If not, where might you take a step to build intentional friendships?

 Growing in the Practice of Justice and Mercy: At the beginning of this practice you assessed where you were at that time. Now assess where you are today.

1. Where have I seen the most movement?
2. Where do I have the most room for growth?

Discussion Prompts and Questions:

1. Review your responses to the Scriptures you've been reading. If you haven't read the Scripture prior to today, read it now and answer the questions together.
2. Share your responses to your questions on peacemaking. Share ways you can encourage each other to not just serve those outside your comfort zone but also to become friends with them.

The Practice of Justice and Mercy—Summary

Discuss before moving on to the next essential practice:

1. What have you learned about the Practice of Justice and Mercy? Where have you seen the most movement? Where do you have the most room for growth?
2. How are you ensuring your actions aren't merely episodic, but that you're moving toward a lifestyle of justice and mercy?
3. Now that you've experimented with some of the accompanying spiritual disciplines, circle the one on which you'll focus for the next thirty days, integrating it into your life:
   - **Serving the poor and marginalized**
   - **Peacemaking**

As a reminder, some spiritual disciplines will be more natural for you, while others will require intentional practice. Over time, you'll find a rhythm that's appropriate to your life stage and spiritual needs.

The Practice of Material Generosity

There is within the human heart a tough fibrous root of fallen life whose nature is to possess, always to possess. It covets "things" with a deep and fierce
passion. The pronouns "my" and "mine" look innocent enough in print, but
their constant and universal use is significant.

—Tozer, The Pursuit of God

Preparation for Your First Meting

Prepare to engage in the Practice of Material Generosity by reading each passage below a few
times. Choose one to commit to memory over the next few weeks.

Psalm 24:1 (NIV) *The earth is the LORD's, and everything in it, the world, and all who live in it.*

2 Corinthians 9:6–7 (NIV) *Remember this: Whoever sows sparingly will also reap sparingly, and
whoever sows generously will also reap generously. Each of you should give what you have decided
in your heart to give, not reluctantly or under compulsion, for God loves a cheerful giver.*

Philippians 4:11–13 (NIV) *I am not` saying this because I am in need, for I have learned to be content
whatever the circumstances. I know what it is to be in need, and I know what it is to have plenty.
I have learned the secret of being content in any and every situation, whether well fed or hungry,
whether living in plenty or in want. I can do everything through him who gives me strength.*

Practice Overview

Read through the following definition of the Practice of Material Generosity. Highlight or underline the words or phrases that stand out to you.

Ordinary disciples of Jesus Christ practice Material Generosity.

Ordinary disciples believe generosity should color all of life and determine their financial decisions. They believe deeply that God owns it all. Followers of Christ are wary of the creeping danger of materialism. They desire to leverage as many resources for the church and God's kingdom as possible and excel at giving. They live their lives under the constant influence of Jesus' teachings on wealth and possessions.

Disciples who practice material generosity are free from the strangling worry of financial bondage. They're also highly productive in God's kingdom mission, able to engage more freely and frequently in His purposes. Ordinary disciples recognize that the biblical guideline of a tithe (10 percent) is a good starting point for generosity, and they take aggressive steps to give 10 percent or more of their material resources to God's kingdom purposes. Disciples who practice material generosity experience the joy of God's love as they excel in this practice.

 Personal Assessment:

I believe that God owns it all.	Strongly Disagree ☐	Somewhat Disagree ☐	Somewhat Agree ☐	Strongly Agree ☐
I currently utilize a personal budget.	Strongly Disagree ☐	Somewhat Disagree ☐	Somewhat Agree ☐	Strongly Agree ☐
I carry an excessive amount of debt.	Strongly Disagree ☐	Somewhat Disagree ☐	Somewhat Agree ☐	Strongly Agree ☐
I gladly share what I have with others.	Strongly Disagree ☐	Somewhat Disagree ☐	Somewhat Agree ☐	Strongly Agree ☐

I live simply so that I have more to share with others.	Strongly Disagree ☐	Somewhat Disagree ☐	Somewhat Agree ☐	Strongly Agree ☐
I regularly give money to support my local church.	Strongly Disagree ☐	Somewhat Disagree ☐	Somewhat Agree ☐	Strongly Agree ☐
I regularly give money to support other ministries.	Strongly Disagree ☐	Somewhat Disagree ☐	Somewhat Agree ☐	Strongly Agree ☐
I would like to be more generous, but my current financial situation keeps me from doing so.	Strongly Disagree ☐	Somewhat Disagree ☐	Somewhat Agree ☐	Strongly Agree ☐

 ## Discussion Prompts and Questions:

1. If someone were to ask you to describe what the Practice of Material Generosity means, what would you say?
2. Give examples of what it's been like for you to practice material generosity throughout your life and discuss some of the obstacles.
3. Share your initial assessment on this practice.

Preparation for Your Second Meeting

 ## Interacting with Scripture

2 Corinthians 8:1–15 (NIV) *And now, brothers, we want you to know about the grace that God has given the Macedonian churches. Out of the most severe trial, their overflowing joy and their extreme poverty welled up in rich generosity. For I testify that they gave as much as they were able, and even beyond their ability. Entirely on their own, they urgently*

Notes:
_____

pleaded with us for the privilege of sharing in this service to the saints. And they did not do as we expected, but they gave themselves first to the Lord and then to us in keeping with God's will. So we urged Titus, since he had earlier made a beginning, to bring also to completion this act of grace on your part. But just as you excel in everything—in faith, in speech, in knowledge, in complete earnestness and in your love for us—see that you also excel in this grace of giving.

I am not commanding you, but I want to test the sincerity of your love by comparing it with the earnestness of others. For you know the grace of our Lord Jesus Christ, that though he was rich, yet for your sakes he became poor, so that you through his poverty might become rich. And here is my advice about what is best for you in this matter: Last year you were the first not only to give but also to have the desire to do so. Now finish the work, so that your eager willingness to do it may be matched by your completion of it, according to your means. For if the willingness is there, the gift is acceptable according to what one has, not according to what he does not have. Our desire is not that others might be relieved while you are hard pressed, but that there might be equality. At the present time your plenty will supply what they need, so that in turn their plenty will supply what you need. Then there will be equality, as it is written: "He who gathered much did not have too much, and he who gathered little did not have too little."

Notes:

1. What does this passage say about material generosity?
2. What does this passage say about God's desire for us to be generous?
3. How would you describe your heart as you consider being generous with your material resources?

The one principle that surrounds everything else is that of stewardship; that we are managers of everything that God has given us.

—Burkett, *The Word on Finances*

 ## Spiritual Disciplines

Over the next few weeks, you'll try some disciplines integral in developing the Practice of Material Generosity:

- **Debt elimination**
- **Personal budgeting**
- **Tithing/giving**
- **Simplicity/asceticism**

 ## Interacting with Scripture

<u>Deuteronomy 15:6 (NLT)</u> *The LORD your God will bless you as he has promised. You will lend money to many nations but will never need to borrow! You will rule many nations, but they will not rule over you!*

<u>Psalms 37:21: (NLT)</u> *The wicked borrow and never repay, but the godly are generous givers.*

<u>Romans 13:8 (NLT)</u> *Pay all your debts, except the debt of love for others. You can never finish paying that! If you love your neighbor, you will fulfill all the requirements of God's law.*

Notes:

1. What stood out to you in the passages?
2. How do the passages convey God's heart toward debt?

Debt elimination is the deliberate process of paying off loans and committing to living without borrowing so as to be free from financial worry and free to contribute generously to God's work.

1. If you're in debt, list three practical steps you can take now to begin moving toward debt elimination.
2. Use the Cascading Debt Elimination System explained at the end of this practice's meeting guide or research Cascading Debt Elimination online for electronic charts and tools.

 ## Interacting with Scripture

Proverbs 6:6–8: (NLT) *Take a lesson from the ants, you lazybones. Learn from their ways and be wise! Even though they have no prince, governor, or ruler to make them work, they labor hard all summer, gathering food for the winter.*

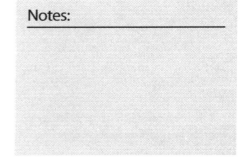

Notes:

Proverbs 27:12: (NLT) A prudent person foresees the danger ahead and takes precautions. The simpleton goes blindly on and suffers the consequences.

1. What stood out to you in the passages?
2. How do the passages convey God's heart toward saving?

 Personal budgeting consists of establishing a planned level of expenditures at a detailed level and sticking to it.

1. If you currently have a personal budget, examine it before your next meeting. Prayerfully consider what needs to stay the same and what may need to change in your budget as you consider the Practice of Material Generosity.
2. If you don't have a personal budget, what's keeping you from taking this step?
3. If you don't have a personal budget, try one of the following:

- Examine a recent time span of thirty days, making note of your household income versus expenses. Check out our resource page for additional online tools to assist you at thewayofdiscipleship.org.
- Visit one of the following websites for ideas on how to create a personal budget: mvelopes.com, mint.com

Discussion Prompts and Questions:

1. Review your responses to the Scriptures you've been reading. If you haven't read the Scripture prior to today, read it now and answer the questions together.
2. Discuss your current debt situation. Do you have a plan to get out of debt? What help do you need for next steps?
3. Discuss your thoughts regarding personal budgeting. To what extent do you include budgeting in the management of household finances?
4. What benefits result for those who plan ahead and set financial goals? What consequences are possible for those who don't?

Preparation for Your Third Meeting

Interacting with Scripture

Malachi 3:8–12 (NIV) *Will a mere mortal rob God? Yet you rob me. "But you ask, 'How are we robbing you?' "In tithes and offerings. You are under a curse—your whole nation— because you are robbing me. Bring the whole tithe into the storehouse, that there may be food in my house. Test me in this," says the Lord Almighty, "and see if I will not throw open the floodgates of heaven and pour out so much blessing that there will not be room enough to store it. I will prevent pests from devouring your crops, and the vines in your fields will not drop their fruit before it is ripe," says the*

Notes:

LORD Almighty. *"Then all the nations will call you blessed, for yours will be a delightful land," says the LORD Almighty.*

Luke 12:16–21 (NIV) *And he told them this parable: "The ground of a certain rich man produced a good crop. He thought to himself, "What shall I do? I have no place to store my crops." Then he said, "This is what I'll do. I will tear down my barns and build bigger ones, and there I will store all my grain and my goods. And I'll say to myself, 'You have plenty of good things laid up for many years. Take life easy; eat, drink and be merry.'" But God said to him, "You fool! This very night your life will be demanded from you. Then who will get what you have prepared for yourself?" This is how it will be with anyone who stores up things for himself but is not rich toward God."*

Notes:

1. What stood out to you in the passages?
2. How do the passages convey God's heart toward tithing/giving?

If enough Christians and others of goodwill will join together at this historic moment, we can end the tragedy of widespread poverty in the richest society on earth. Indeed, we could dramatically reduce poverty around the world. If that happens, future historians will call us the Generous Christians Generation.

—Sider, *Just Generosity*

Tithing/giving is the setting aside of at least 10 percent of your gross income to be given to your church (5 percent or half) and other kingdom-serving organizations (the other 5 percent or half). Ten percent is a good starting point from which generosity can grow.

1. What would be the value of including your tithe in your personal budget? What will likely be the result if tithing isn't part of your plan?

2. While giving 10 percent of your gross income may not be currently possible, prayerfully consider increasing the percentage you are giving by 1 percent or more each year. Reflect this change in your personal budget.

 ## Interacting with Scripture

Matthew 5:3 (NIV): *Blessed are the poor in spirit, for theirs is the kingdom of heaven.*

Matthew 16:24–25 (NLT) *Then Jesus said to his disciples, "If any of you wants to be my follower, you must turn from your selfish ways, take up your cross, and follow me. [25] If you try to hang on to your life, you will lose it. But if you give up your life for my sake, you will save it."*

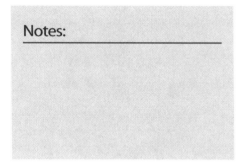
Notes:

1. Why do you think God desires for us to live without excess? What might be the result of sacrificially relinquishing something that consumes your time, thoughts, and heart?
2. Prayerfully consider what *you* might sacrificially surrender in your own life for a season. What might you sacrificially surrender for *good*?
3. Now pray the following prayer by A.W. Tozer:
   Father, I want to know Thee, but my coward heart fears to give up its toys. I cannot part with them without inward bleeding, and I do not try to hide from Thee the terror of the parting. I come trembling, but I do come. Please root from my heart all those things which I have cherished so long and which have become a very part of my living self, so that Thou mayest enter and dwell there without a rival. Then shalt Thou make the place of Thy feet glorious. Then shall my heart have no need of the sun to shine in it, for Thyself wilt be the light of it, and there shall be no night there. In Jesus' Name, Amen. (2013)

Simplicity is the choice to scale down the consumption and busyness of life, living purposely with less and choosing to do less. It's a state of being freed from complexity, luxury, pretentiousness, and ornamentation. Asceticism is a more extreme form of simplicity characterized by a sacrificial lifestyle.

1. What area of your life do you most need to simplify (possessions, time commitments, social obligations, financial expenditures, entertainment, technology, media, etc.)?
2. In a prayer below, ask the Lord for help to practice simplicity in order to have more space in your life to be aware of and responsive to Him. Be specific, offering Him at least one area of your life you hope to simplify.

Father,

 Growing in the Practice of Material Generosity: At the beginning of this practice you assessed where you were at that time. Now assess where you are today. Where have I seen the most movement?

1. Where have I seen the most personal growth in this practice?
2. Where do I have the most room for growth?

 Discussion Prompts and Questions:

1. Review your responses to the Scriptures you've been reading. If you haven't read the Scripture prior to today, read it now and answer the questions together.
2. Discuss where you are in your journey toward generosity. Share with one another what barriers you face and what steps you're taking to be more generous with the discipline of tithing/giving.
3. Discuss your thoughts regarding the spiritual discipline of simplicity/asceticism. Was this spiritual discipline new to you? How might you incorporate it into your life?

The Practice of Material Generosity—Summary

Discuss before moving on to the next essential practice:

1. What have you learned about the Practice of Material Generosity?
2. In what areas of your life is God calling you to adjust in order to continue to move toward material generosity? Where have you seen the most movement? Where do you have the most room for growth?
3. Now that you've experimented with some of the spiritual disciplines accompanying material generosity, circle one to focus on over the next thirty days:
   - **Personal budgeting**
   - **Tithing/giving**
   - **Debt elimination**
   - **Simplicity/asceticism**

Cascading Debt Destroyer

The System—It's possible to become totally debt free in five to seven years. Follow these seven steps and it'll happen for you.

1. Prioritize your debts. Use the formula given below.
2. Make the minimum required monthly payments on all debts except the highest priority debt.
3. Add the entire Accelerator Amount to the regular payment on the highest priority debt.
4. Continue this process until the first debt is paid off.
5. After debt number one is paid off, move on to the second debt on your priority list. You'll now have your initial Accelerator Amount plus the payment you were making on the first debt to add to the payoff of the second debt.
6. Repeat again and again, moving down your debt priority list.
7. On average, people pay off their credit cards and cars in the first one to two years and then they can typically pay off their mortgage in four to five years.

Accelerator Amount—Begin with the Accelerator Amount (A). This is the additional amount of money that you need to apply to the payoff of your debts each month. To begin with, try to apply 10 percent of your take-home pay to debt elimination. For example if you bring home $3000 try to apply $300. If you don't know where to get this additional Accelerator Amount, try to see if you have any debts that could be consolidated to lower payments. Many times, people are paying interest rates on their existing debts that are too high, and they can find the extra amount they need just by consolidating and shrinking some existing payments. Usually, the mortgage payment or home equity lines of credit can be used for this purpose. You should constantly be trying to find ways to increase your Accelerator Amount. The faster you can become debt free, the sooner you can become financially independent.

The Formula—The formula for prioritizing your debts is as follows:
- Column 1—Write down all of your debts, anything that has a balance you're working to pay off.
- Column 2—Write down the balance.
- Column 3—Write down the minimum payment—exclude taxes and insurance.
- Column 4—Divide Column 2 by Column 3.
- Column 5—Start with the lowest value in Column 4 as priority debt number one and work your way up to the largest value in Column 4.
- Column 6—Add the Accelerator Amount to the minimum payment of debt priority number one, then add that total to debt priority number 2 and so on.
- Column 7—Divide Column 2 by Column 6 in order to see the approximate months it would take to pay off your debt.

Let's see how much you currently owe. Add all of the values in Column 2 and write that on your worksheet (B). Just look at how much you're paying each month to those creditors. Simply add all the answers in Column 3 and write that value on your worksheet (C). Finally, add your Accelerator Amount to your total monthly payments and write that on your worksheet (A+C=D). Utilize the included Cascading Debt Destroyer Map to visualize how quickly you can be debt free.

The Results—By following the steps outlined you'll become debt-free. Realize that the barriers to reaching your financial independence are your current debts, and you'll be well on your way to reaching your goals.

Cascading Debt Destroyer Worksheet

Accelerator Amount (A): _____

Debt	Balance	Monthly Payment	Division Answer	Payoff Priority	Acc. Payment	Months to Pay Off
Column 1	Column 2	Column 3	Column 4	Column 5	Column 6	Column 7

Total Debt (B)

_____

Total Monthly Payments (C)

_____

Total Accelerated Payments (A+C)

_____

The Practice of Loving Others Well

> We've come to view love as being "nice," yet the kind of love modeled by
> Jesus Christ has nothing to do with manners or unconditional acceptance.
> Rather, it is disruptive, courageous, and socially unacceptable.
>
> —Allender, Bold Love

Preparation for Your First Meeting

Prepare to engage in the Practice of Loving Others Well by reading each passage below a few times. Choose one to commit to memory over the next few weeks.

John 13:34–35 (NIV) A new command I give you: Love one another. As I have loved you, so you must love one another. By this everyone will know that you are my disciples, if you love one another.

1 John 3:16–18 (NLT) We know what real love is because Jesus gave up his life for us. So we also ought to give up our lives for our brothers and sisters. If someone has enough money to live well and sees a brother or sister in need but shows no compassion—how can God's love be in that person? Dear children, let's not merely say that we love each other; let us show the truth by our actions.

The goal of discipleship is love—love God and love others. When you observe growth in your love for others, you are moving toward Christ. How will "everyone" know that you are a disciple of Jesus?

 Practice Overview

Read through the following definition of the Practice of Loving Others Well. Highlight or underline the words or phrases that stand out to you.

> **Ordinary disciples of Jesus Christ love others well.**
> Ordinary disciples of Jesus Christ believe it's their responsibility to love others in the same manner Christ loves them. Their deepest desires are fueled by the passion to love others well. They strive to know others enough to accurately offer the kind of love needed in the moment—compassion, care, forgiveness, and rebuke. Disciples of Jesus practice the Biblical "one anothers," and their lives reflect the interdependence that exemplifies all followers of Jesus.
>
> When disciples of Jesus love in this manner, God uncovers and deals with sin, comforts those in mourning, heals the sick, welcomes the lonely, reconciles those at odds, liberates those under spiritual bondage, and gives guidance to the lost. Disciples who love others well will experience the joy of a life centered on God's high priority of bringing wholeness to others.

 Personal Assessment:

	Almost Never	Rarely	Occasionally	Frequently	Consistently	Not Sure
God helps me to help others deal with uncovered sin.	☐	☐	☐	☐	☐	☐
God enables me to comfort those who mourn.	☐	☐	☐	☐	☐	☐
God empowers me to heal the sick.	☐	☐	☐	☐	☐	☐
God works through me to liberate others in spiritual bondage.	☐	☐	☐	☐	☐	☐
God uses me to give the lost guidance.	☐	☐	☐	☐	☐	☐
I experience the joy of a life centered on God's high priority of bringing wholeness to others.	☐	☐	☐	☐	☐	☐

Discussion Prompts and Questions:

1. If someone were to ask you to describe what the Practice of Loving Others Well means, how would you respond?
2. Who has loved you well? Give examples of how this person practiced loving others well.
3. Share your initial assessment on this practice.
4. What are some examples of ways you have or are loving others well?

 Interacting with Scripture

Matthew 22:36–40 (NIV) *"Teacher, which is the most important commandment in the law of Moses?" Jesus replied, "'You must love the Lord your God with all your heart, all your soul, and all your mind.' This is the first and greatest commandment. A second is equally important: 'Love your neighbor as yourself.' The entire law and all the demands of the prophets are based on these two commandments."*

Notes:

1 John 4:20–21 (NASB) *If someone says, "I love God," and hates his brother, he is a liar; for he who does not love his brother whom he has seen, how can he love God whom he has not seen? And this commandment we have from him: that he who loves God must love his brother also.*

1. What do these passages tell us about loving others well?
2. What's the connection between loving God and loving others? Why is this connection so strong?
3. Who is your "neighbor"? Do you struggle with loving your neighbor as yourself? What makes it difficult for you to love others?

To pray, "God, please help my neighbor cope with her financial problems," or, "God, do something about the homeless downtown," is the approach of a theist, not a Christian. God has chosen to express love and grace in the world through those of us who embody Christ.

—Yancey, *Prayer*

 ## Spiritual Disciplines

Over the next few weeks, you'll experiment with some of the disciplines integral in developing the Practice of Loving Others Well:

- **Intercessory prayer**
- **Hospitality**
- **Accountability**
- **Purposeful community**

 Intercessory prayer is spending time praying directly for the people around us who are far from Jesus and asking God to reveal ways we can engage them in the conversation.

Prayer is the action of love. It's being attentive to their needs. It's choosing to take those needs to God and speaking on their behalf. Intercessory prayer is time spent with God that can change you as you express love for others. This spiritual discipline includes setting aside time daily as well as immediate prayers in critical situations.

Set aside fifteen minutes before you're together again to practice intercessory prayer using the guide below:

God, I hold in Your healing presence those who suffer pain and ill health...

Father, I hold in Your healing presence those who suffer in mind and spirit...

God, I hold in Your healing presence the suffering people of our world, and the places where people are experiencing hurt and division, including places of hurt and division in my own life...

Father, I hold in Your healing presence those experiencing grief and loss...

God, I hold in Your healing presence those who need wisdom for their next steps...

Father, I hold in Your healing presence those people and situations that seem broken beyond repair...

Loving God, I hold in Your healing presence and peace those whose needs are not known to me but are known by You, and those for whom I've been asked to pray...

And I name in my heart all those who are close to me...

May they know the deep peace of Christ. Amen[5]

 Hospitality is inviting others into our homes and lives, to build relationships and natural opportunities to share our lives and faith.

Hospitality is usually defined as a meal together or providing a place to stay the night. However, it's so much more than that. It's kindness in welcoming guests and strangers. It's receptivity to others with whom you come in contact. It's being attentive to others. Being hospitable is creating space in your life to really see people—their hopes, dreams, and needs—and love them.

Who do you need to create space for? What practical ways will you show hospitality?

This spiritual discipline requires margin in your life to invite others to know you and your relationship with God. Choose one relationship in which to show God's love this week. Write down that person's name.

---

5   Ruth Haley Barton, *Strengthening the Soul of Your Leadership: Seeking God in the Crucible of Ministry*. Downers Grove: InterVarsity Press, 2008.

Preparation for Your Second Meeting

 ### Interacting with Scripture

1 Corinthians 13:4–8a (NLT) *Love is patient, love is kind. It does not envy, it does not boast, it is not proud. It does not dishonor others, it is not self-seeking, it is not easily angered, it keeps no record of wrongs. Love does not delight in evil but rejoices with the truth. It always protects, always trusts, always hopes, always perseveres. Love never fails.*

Romans 13:8–10 (NLT) *Owe nothing to anyone—except for your obligation to love one another. If you love your neighbor, you will fulfill the requirements of God's law. For the commandments say, "You must not commit adultery. You must not murder. You must not steal. You must not covet." These—and other such commandments—are summed up in this one commandment: "Love your neighbor as yourself." Love does no wrong to others, so love fulfills the requirements of God's law.*

1 Peter 4:8–10 (NIV) *Above all, love each other deeply, because love covers over a multitude of sins. Offer hospitality to one another without grumbling. Each of you should use whatever gift you have received to serve others, as faithful stewards of God's grace in its various forms.*

Notes: _____

1. Review your responses to the Scriptures you've been reading. If you haven't read the Scripture prior to today, read it now and answer the questions together.
2. In what ways does love cover sins? What does the role of grace (unmerited favor from God) play in loving others well?

3. Which of the descriptions of love in 1 Corinthians 13 are most difficult for you?

4. Although loving someone in this manner can be difficult, it's possible. How is expressing this kind of love possible? To whom do you need to show this kind of love?

 ## Discussion Prompts and Questions:

1. What are you learning about the importance of loving others well?

2. Describe your experience with the spiritual disciplines of intercessory prayer and hospitality. What did you notice about loving others well as you engaged in these spiritual disciplines?

3. How do you see yourself growing in love? In which of your own relationships are you especially challenged to show love? Why?

4. In what relationships do you see yourself growing in loving others well?

Preparation for Your Third Meeting

 ## Interacting with Scripture

Galatians 6:2–5 (NIV) *Carry each other's burdens, and in this way you will fulfill the law of Christ. If anyone thinks they are something when they are not, they deceive themselves. Each one should test their own actions. Then they can take pride in themselves alone, without comparing themselves to someone else, for each one should carry their own load.*

Colossians 3:12–16 (NLT) *Since God chose you to be the holy people he loves; you must clothe yourselves with tenderhearted mercy, kindness, humility, gentleness, and patience. Make allowance for each other's faults, and forgive anyone who offends you. Remember, the Lord forgave you, so you must forgive others. Above all, clothe yourselves with love, which binds us all together in perfect harmony. And let the peace that comes from Christ rule in your hearts.*

Notes:

For as members of one body you are called to live in peace. And always be thankful. Let the message about Christ, in all its richness, fill your lives. Teach and counsel each other with all the wisdom he gives. Sing psalms and hymns and spiritual songs to God with thankful hearts.

1. The proper translation of Galatians 6 suggests that a burden can feel like a ten-ton boulder while a load feels like a ten-pound rock. What does it look like to help carry another's burden? Can you think of a time another person helped carry your burden?
2. What's loving about encouraging others to carry their own loads?
3. What role does forgiveness play in loving others well? What's your motivation to forgive?
4. From these passages, when love is present, so is peace. In what relationship(s) do *you* need more peace?

The Bible knows nothing of solitary religion.

—John Wesley

 Accountability is resolving to engage in relationships with others for the purpose of providing an honest perspective and rebuke, when necessary.

Who in your life holds you accountable? Have you given anyone permission to provide honest feedback and tell you the truth?

Is there a particular relationship or circumstance where you need someone to help you see more clearly?

This week, ask God to provide someone in your life to help hold you accountable. If He brings someone to mind, consider asking that person if he or she would be your accountability partner.

Purposeful community is intentionally sharing life with a small group of people for study, prayer, care, and accountability.

Are you in an intentional community? If not, where might you take a step to build intentional friendships?

 Interacting with Scripture

Ephesians 4:15 (NIV) *Instead, speaking the truth in love, we will grow to become in every respect the mature body of Him who is the head that is Christ.*

2 Timothy 3:16–17 (NLT) *All Scripture is inspired by God and is useful to teach us what's true and to make us realize what's wrong in our lives. It corrects us when we are wrong and teaches us to do what's right. God uses it to prepare and equip his people to do every good work.*

Matthew 18:15–20: (NLT) *If another believer sins against you, go privately and point out the offense. If the other person listens and confesses it, you have won that person back. But if you are unsuccessful, take one or two others with you and go back again, so that everything you say may be confirmed by two or three witnesses. If the person still refuses to listen, take your case to the church. Then if he or she won't accept the church's decision, treat that person as a pagan or a corrupt tax collector.*

Notes:

I tell you the truth, whatever you forbid on earth will be forbidden in heaven, and whatever you permit on earth will be permitted in heaven. I also tell you this: If two of you agree here on earth concerning anything you ask, my Father in heaven will do it for you. For where two or three gather together as my followers, I am there among them.

Notes:

1. What's loving about telling the truth?
2. Why does Scripture give us such specific instructions regarding "offenses"? What's been your experience when someone has honestly told you how you offended him or her? When have you gone to another about an offense against you? What was the result?
3. What's the outcome of loving others well through conflict? Why do we often run away from these kinds of encounters? Who are you avoiding today in order to escape conflict?

 Growing in the Practice of Loving Others Well: At the beginning of this practice you assessed where you were at that time. Now assess where you are today.

1. Where have I seen the most personal growth in this practice?
2. Where do I have the most room for growth?

 Discussion Prompts and Questions:

1. Review your responses to the Scriptures you've been reading. If you haven't read the Scripture prior to today, read it now and answer the questions together.

2. Discuss relationships that still need improvement in your life.
3. What have you learned about the Practice of Loving Others Well? Where have you seen the most movement? Where do you have the most room for growth?
4. What was the most difficult thing for you as you considered these spiritual disciplines?

The Practice of Loving Others Well—Summary

Answer these questions and discuss before moving on to the next essential practice:

1. What have you learned about the Practice of Loving Others Well?
2. How are you ensuring that you're moving toward a lifestyle of loving others well?
3. Now that you've experimented with some of the accompanying spiritual disciplines, circle the one on which you'll focus for the next thirty days by integrating it into your life:
   - **Intercessory prayer**
   - **Hospitality**
   - **Accountability**
   - **Purposeful community**

As a reminder, some spiritual disciplines will be more natural for you, while others will require intentional practice. Over time, you'll find a rhythm that's appropriate to your life stage and spiritual needs.

The Practice of Leading Others to Jesus

> If you're not a bold evangelist, you're in the majority. In fact, you're in great company—including Saint Peter, the ultimate Green Beret who became the world's biggest Christian chicken.
>
> —Henderson, Evangelism Without Additives

Preparation for Your First Meeting

Prepare to engage in the Practice of Leading Others to Jesus by reading each passage below a few times.

<u>Isaiah 52:7 (NIV)</u> *How beautiful on the mountains are the feet of those who bring good news, who proclaim peace, who bring good tidings, who proclaim salvation, who say to Zion, "Your God reigns!"*

<u>2 Corinthians 5:20 (NIV)</u> *We are therefore Christ's ambassadors, as though God were making His appeal through us. We implore you on Christ's behalf: Be reconciled to God.*

<u>Acts 1:8 (NIV)</u> *But you will receive power when the Holy Spirit comes on you; and you will be my witnesses in Jerusalem, and in all Judea and Samaria, and to the ends of the earth.*

 Practice Overview

Read through the following definition of the Practice of Leading Others to Jesus. Highlight or underline the words or phrases that stand out to you.

Ordinary disciples of Jesus Christ lead others to follow Jesus.
They believe faith in Jesus is the most important aspect of life—so much so that they relentlessly share the Gospel of Christ in both word and deed. They passionately believe God's Spirit can change anyone's life to reflect the life of Jesus, and this conviction leads them to fervently pray for and serve lost and broken people. Ordinary disciples of Jesus see all of life as an opportunity to lead others to Jesus.

Disciples who live with a relentless desire to lead lost people to Jesus experience the joy of engaging with others about new life. They know the wonder of seeing the miracle of Spirit-changed lives. Christ followers have the satisfaction that grows out of participating in this important kingdom purpose, given to all disciples by Jesus, as those far from God are reconciled to Him and become followers of Jesus.

 Personal Assessment:

I'm convicted that sharing the Good News is the most important gift I can give to another.	Strongly Disagree ☐	Somewhat Disagree ☐	Somewhat Agree ☐	Strongly Agree ☐		
I'm confident in sharing the Good News with people in my spheres of influence.	Strongly Disagree ☐	Somewhat Disagree ☐	Somewhat Agree ☐	Strongly Agree ☐		
I pray specifically for friends, neighbors, coworkers, and/or family who don't know Christ.	Almost Never ☐	Rarely ☐	Occasionally ☐	Frequently ☐	Consistently ☐	Not Sure ☐
I look for ways to build relationships with people who don't know Christ.	Almost Never ☐	Rarely ☐	Occasionally ☐	Frequently ☐	Consistently ☐	Not Sure ☐

Write out your story of faith in Christ. Be prepared to share it at your meeting.

1. What was the story that led you to follow Jesus Christ?
2. What hurdles did you have to overcome in order to fully give your life to Jesus Christ?
3. How has Jesus Christ changed your life?
4. How would you describe your current relationship with Jesus Christ?

 ## Discussion Prompts and Questions:

1. If someone were to ask you to describe what's meant by the Practice of Leading Others to Jesus, what would you say?
2. Give examples of what it's been like for you to practice leading others to Jesus throughout your life and discuss some of the obstacles.
3. Share your initial assessment on this practice.
4. Discuss your responses to the questions related to your faith story.

 ## Interacting with Scripture

Luke 15 (NIV) *Now the tax collectors and sinners were all gathering around to hear Jesus. But the Pharisees and the teachers of the law muttered, "This man welcomes sinners and eats with them."*

Notes:

Then Jesus told them this parable: "Suppose one of you has a hundred sheep and loses one of them. Doesn't he leave the ninety-nine in the open country and go after the lost sheep until he finds it? And when he finds it, he joyfully puts it on his shoulders and goes home. Then he calls his friends and neighbors together and says, 'Rejoice with me; I have found my lost sheep.' I tell you that in the same way there will be more rejoicing in heaven over one sinner who repents than over ninety-nine righteous persons who do not need to repent.

Or suppose a woman has ten silver coins and loses one. Doesn't she light a lamp, sweep the house and search carefully until she finds it? And when she finds it, she calls her friends and neighbors together and says, 'Rejoice with me; I have found my lost coin.' In the same way, I tell you, there is rejoicing in the presence of the angels of God over one sinner who repents."

Jesus continued: "There was a man who had two sons. The younger one said to his father, 'Father, give me my share of the estate.' So he divided his property between them.

Not long after that, the younger son got together all he had, set off for a distant country and there squandered his wealth in wild living. After he had spent everything, there was a severe famine in that whole country, and he began to be in need. So he went and hired himself out to a citizen of that country, who sent him to his fields to feed pigs. He longed to fill his stomach with the pods that the pigs were eating, but no one gave him anything.

When he came to his senses, he said, 'How many of my father's hired servants have food to spare, and here I am starving to death! I will set out and go back to my father and say to him: Father, I have sinned against heaven and against you. I am no longer worthy to be called your son; make me like one of your hired servants.' So he got up and went to his father.

But while he was still a long way off, his father saw him and was filled with compassion for him; he ran to his son, threw his arms around him and kissed him.

The son said to him, 'Father, I have sinned against heaven and against you. I am no longer worthy to be called your son.'

Notes: _____

But the father said to his servants, 'Quick! Bring the best robe and put it on him. Put a ring on his finger and sandals on his feet. Bring the fattened calf and kill it. Let's have a feast and celebrate. For this son of mine was dead and is alive again; he was lost and is found.' So they began to celebrate.

Meanwhile, the older son was in the field. When he came near the house, he heard music and dancing. So he called one of the servants and asked him what was going on. 'Your brother has come,' he replied, 'and your father has killed the fattened calf because he has him back safe and sound.'

The older brother became angry and refused to go in. So his father went out and pleaded with him. But he answered his father, 'Look! All these years I've been slaving for you and never disobeyed your orders. Yet you never gave me even a young goat so I could celebrate with my friends. But when this son of yours who has squandered your property with prostitutes comes home, you kill the fattened calf for him!'

'My son,' the father said, 'you are always with me, and everything I have is yours. But we had to celebrate and be glad, because this brother of yours was dead and is alive again; he was lost and is found.'"

1. What do we learn about God from these three stories?
2. How much does your heart reflect God's heart for those who are lost?

Notes:

Spiritual Disciplines

Over the next few weeks, you'll experiment with some of the disciplines integral in developing the Practice of Leading Others to Jesus:

- **Studying the Bible and apologetics**
- **Intercessory prayer**
- **Hospitality**
- **Intentional friendships**

 Studying the Bible and apologetics involves taking time to understand what we believe and why, so as to be able to convey this to others.

Preparation for Your Second Meeting

 Interacting with Scripture

Matthew 9:35–38 (NIV) *Jesus went through all the towns and villages, teaching in their synagogues, proclaiming the good news of the kingdom and healing every disease and sickness. When he saw the crowds, he had compassion on them, because they were harassed and helpless, like sheep without a shepherd. Then he said to his disciples, "The harvest is plentiful but the workers are few. Ask the Lord of the harvest, therefore, to send out workers into his harvest field."*

Matthew 28:16–20 (NIV) *Then the eleven disciples went to Galilee, to the mountain where Jesus had told them to go. When they saw him, they worshiped him; but some doubted. Then Jesus came to them and said, "All authority in heaven and on earth has been given to me. Therefore go and make*

Notes:

disciples of all nations, baptizing them in the name of the Father and of the Son and of the Holy Spirit, and teaching them to obey everything I have commanded you. And surely I am with you always, to the very end of the age."

Notes:

1. What role did Jesus envision for his disciples?
2. What specifically did Jesus ask his disciples to do?
3. Who in your life is "harassed and helpless"?

What if redirecting a person's forever really is as simple as walking across a room?

—Hybels, *Just Walk Across the Room*

 Intercessory prayer is spending time praying directly for the people around us who are far from Jesus and asking God to reveal ways we can engage them in the conversation.

Before your next meeting, write down the names of three people who haven't surrendered their lives to Jesus. Commit to pray for them regularly throughout the rest of this practice.

 Hospitality is inviting others into our homes and lives, to build relationships and natural opportunities to share our lives and faith.

Consider inviting one of those three people over for a meal or an evening together in your home.

Jesus is not a pathway to an easy life but a call to do hard things if we are to live in the image of our Lord. "Love my enemies?" "Give my riches to the poor and take up the cross?" "Die so that I might live?"

—Ortberg, *Who Is This Man?*

Discussion Prompts and Questions:

1. What stood out to you from Matthew 9 and Matthew 28?
2. What roles do the disciplines of prayer and hospitality play in leading others to Jesus?
3. What people have you started praying for? Discuss any significant interaction you had with them.

 ## Interacting with Scripture

John 3:16 (NIV) *For God so loved the world that he gave his one and only Son, that whoever believes in him shall not perish but have eternal life.*

1 Corinthians 15:3–8 (NIV) *For what I received I passed on to you as of first importance: that Christ died for our sins according to the Scriptures, that he was buried, that he was raised on the third day according to the Scriptures, and that he appeared to Cephas, and then to the Twelve. After that, he appeared to more than five hundred of the brothers and sisters at the same time, most of whom are still living, though some have fallen asleep. Then he appeared to James, then to all the apostles, and last of all he appeared to me also, as to one abnormally born.*

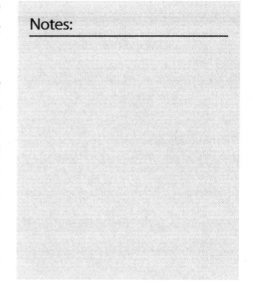

Notes:

1. What's the essence of the Gospel (Good News)?
2. How desperate should we be to share the Good News with those who haven't surrendered their lives to Jesus? What are the consequences for those who haven't heard or don't respond?
3. How desperate are you? Who brought the Good News to you?

Preparation for Your Third Meeting

 Interacting with Scripture

Romans 10:10–15 (NIV) *For it is with your heart that you believe and are justified, and it is with your mouth that you profess your faith and are saved. As Scripture says, "Anyone who believes in him will never be put to shame." For there is no difference between Jew and Gentile—the same Lord is Lord of all and richly blesses all who call on him, for, "Everyone who calls on the name of the Lord will be saved."*

How, then, can they call on the one they have not believed in? And how can they believe in the one of whom they have not heard? And how can they hear without someone preaching to them? And how can anyone preach unless they are sent? As it is written: "How beautiful are the feet of those who bring good news!"

1 Peter 3:15–16 (NIV) *But in your hearts revere Christ as Lord. Always be prepared to give an answer to everyone who asks you to give the reason for the hope that you have. But do this with gentleness and respect, keeping a clear conscience, so that those who speak maliciously against your good behavior in Christ may be ashamed of their slander.*

1 Corinthians 9:19–23 (NIV) *Though I am free and belong to no one, I have made myself a slave to everyone, to win as many as possible. To the Jews I became like a Jew, to win the Jews. To those under the law I became like one under the law (though I myself am not under the law), so as to win those under the law. To those not having the law I became*

Notes:

like one not having the law (though I am not free from God's law but am under Christ's law), so as to win those not having the law. To the weak I became weak, to win the weak. I have become all things to all people so that by all possible means I might save some. I do all this for the sake of the gospel that I may share in its blessings.

Notes:

1. What stood out to you in these passages?
2. How can you use your natural experiences, personality, and giftedness to share the Good News?
3. What are some of the principles these passages speak of in sharing the Good News?

 Intentional friendships is the practice of engaging in natural relationships with those in our lives (work, neighborhood, community, and family) so as to have the opportunity to lead them to Jesus.

1. Think of the three people you've been praying for. Ask God to lead you to focus on one of them. Contemplate your relationship with that person and what you know about him or her. Through prayer and listening to God, ask for discernment and insight into that person's life. Ask God to show you how to have a conversation about the Good News with this person. Think of the questions you could ask to begin this conversation.
2. Plan a way to naturally have this conversation in the next two weeks. Incorporate some of your own faith story in your conversation.

 Growing in the Practice of Leading Others to Jesus: At the beginning of this practice you assessed where you were at that time. Now assess where you are.

1. Where have I seen the most movement?
2. Where do I have the most room for growth?

Discussion Prompts and Questions:

1. Review your responses to the Scriptures you've been reading. If you haven't read the Scripture prior to today, read it now and answer the questions together.
2. Share what God revealed to you about the person with whom you're committing to share the Good News.
3. What fears do you have in sharing the Good News with that person? Spend some time praying together about those fears.
4. What have you learned about the Practice of Leading Others to Jesus? Where have you seen the most movement? Where do you have the most room for growth?

Interacting with Scripture

2 Timothy 1:7 (NIV) *For the Spirit God gave us does not make us timid, but gives us power, love and self-discipline.*

1 Thessalonians 1:4–5 (NIV, 84) *For we know, brothers loved by God, that he has chosen you, because our gospel came to you not simply with words, but also with power, with the Holy Spirit and with deep conviction. You know how we lived among you for your sake.*

Romans 1:16 (NIV, 84) *I am not ashamed of the gospel, because it is the power of God for the salvation of everyone who believes: first for the Jew, then for the Gentile.*

2 Corinthians 12:9–10 (NIV) *My grace is sufficient for you, for my power is made perfect in weakness. Therefore I will boast all the more gladly about my weaknesses, so that Christ's power may rest on me. That is why, for Christ's sake, I delight in weaknesses, in insults, in hardships, in persecutions, in difficulties. For when I am weak, then I am strong.*

Notes:
_____

1. What do these passages tell us about our fears?
2. What's God saying to you?

The Practice of Leading Others to Jesus—Summary

1. What have you learned about the Practice of Leading Others to Jesus?
2. How are you ensuring that your actions aren't merely episodic, but that you're moving toward a lifestyle of leading others to Jesus?
3. Now that you've experimented with some of the accompanying spiritual disciplines, circle the one on which you'll focus for the next thirty days, integrating it into your life:
   - **Studying the Bible and apologetics**
   - **Intercessory prayer**
   - **Hospitality**
   - **Intentional friendships**

Passing the Baton

> By Jesus' multiplication of himself in the Twelve, they would geographically cover far greater territory than he ever did in his limited itinerant ministry. By the power of the indwelling Holy Spirit carrying them to the entire known world, the sheer volume of Jesus' ministry would expand exponentially. And so it has been.
>
> —Ogden, Transforming Discipleship

Preparation for Your First Meeting

One of the goals of every discipleship relationship is for each disciple to eventually disciple someone else.

Determining whether you're ready to launch your own discipleship relationship is an art, not a science. You might be ready to begin leading your own disciple within the context of your existing relationship (both relationships happening concurrently).

If you've walked through a few of the practices with your discipler, and you both agree that you've arrived at the point where you're able to intentionally lead someone, then go for it! Or you may not be ready to begin leading your own discipleship relationship until you've fully integrated all eleven practices.

In order to get ready to begin your own discipleship relationship, strategically focus on the Practice of Leading Others to Jesus. This practice serves as a great launching pad into the conversation regarding beginning a discipleship relationship. *Leading Others to Jesus* isn't just about leading people to Christ for the first time but also about your development as a follower of Christ. In fact, your present relationship with your discipler is part of this larger practice.

Jesus and Paul made strong statements throughout Scripture about the need to make and multiply disciples:

Interacting with Scripture

<u>2 Timothy 2:1–2 (NIV)</u> *You then, my son, be strong in the grace that is in Christ Jesus. And the things you have heard me say in the presence of many witnesses entrust to reliable people who will also be qualified to teach others.*

<u>Matthew 28:18–20 (NIV)</u> *Then Jesus came to them and said, "All authority in heaven and on earth has been given to me. Therefore go and make disciples of all nations, baptizing them in the name of the Father and of the Son and of the Holy Spirit, and teaching them to obey everything I have commanded you. And surely I am with you always, to the very end of the age."*

Notes:

1. What stood out to you in these passages?
2. What does it mean to you that Jesus would entrust you to share in His mission?

 Ready to disciple another? Here's a personal assessment to review with your discipler.

	Strongly Disagree	Somewhat Disagree	Somewhat Agree	Strongly Agree
I've studied and integrated many of the eleven practices into my daily life.	☐	☐	☐	☐
I have a good understanding of the Practice of Leading Others to Jesus.	☐	☐	☐	☐

I've approached my current discipleship relationship with commitment.	Almost Never ☐	Rarely ☐	Occasionally ☐	Frequently ☐	Consistently ☐	Not Sure ☐

I've taken the training to be a discipler either live or online.	Yes ☐	No ☐

 Discussion Prompts and Questions:

1. Review what you learned from your study.
2. Review your assessment with your discipler. Compare notes.
3. If it's time to "pass the baton," talk about how your discipleship relationship should come to an end.

Preparation for Your Second Meeting

Here are some ideas of what to do as well as what to discuss together.

*   Discuss how you want to celebrate the "passing of the baton". Ideas: go out to dinner to celebrate or go on an overnight retreat.
*   Review your time together.
*   Take the assessment again on the eleven practices. Discuss growth or movement over your time together.
*   Remember the highlights from your time together.
*   Talk about what your relationship will look like following this "intentional, time-bound relationship."
*   Have a time of prayer and commissioning together to pass the baton.

Personal Assessment

The following assessment will help the discipler and disciple determine to what extent the eleven practices are currently part of their daily lives. Read through the description of each practice, then complete the assessment. Plan to discuss it together the next time you meet.

How frequently do you engage in these practices?

	Almost Never	Rarely	Occasionally	Frequently	Consistently
Ordinary disciples of Jesus Christ practice surrender to God and trust in Him.	☐	☐	☐	☐	☐
Ordinary disciples of Jesus Christ practice disengagement from their routines and distractions in order to commune with God.	☐	☐	☐	☐	☐
Ordinary disciples of Jesus Christ study the Word of God and take in good Biblical teaching that will transform their lives.	☐	☐	☐	☐	☐
Ordinary disciples of Jesus Christ engage in lifestyles of justice and mercy.	☐	☐	☐	☐	☐
Ordinary disciples of Jesus Christ seek the call of God on their lives.	☐	☐	☐	☐	☐
Ordinary disciples of Jesus Christ practice self-denial.	☐	☐	☐	☐	☐
Ordinary disciples of Jesus Christ are committed to living in spiritual communities through local churches.	☐	☐	☐	☐	☐

Ordinary disciples of Jesus Christ practice moral integrity.	Almost Never ☐	Rarely ☐	Occasionally ☐	Frequently ☐	Consistently ☐
Ordinary disciples of Jesus Christ practice material generosity.	Almost Never ☐	Rarely ☐	Occasionally ☐	Frequently ☐	Consistently ☐
Ordinary disciples of Jesus Christ love others well.	Almost Never ☐	Rarely ☐	Occasionally ☐	Frequently ☐	Consistently ☐
Ordinary disciples of Jesus Christ lead others to follow Jesus.	Almost Never ☐	Rarely ☐	Occasionally ☐	Frequently ☐	Consistently ☐

Discipler Resources

Relationships

The Discipler

 What does it mean to be a discipler?

A discipler is someone who's invited a person into a directive, intentional relationship that explores the eleven practices of an ordinary follower of Christ. Rather than simply being responsive in this relationship, a discipler's investment into the life of another includes two things:

1. A plan of the direction he or she wants to lead the discipled.
2. Specific, anticipated outcomes of time spent together as discipler and discipled.

Disciplers will have the confidence to lead others in incorporating the eleven practices of an ordinary follower of Christ because they're already doing so in their own lives. The discipler's role isn't to tell a person what to do, but rather to walk alongside the disciple as the discipled figures out what he or she has already been told by Jesus and to then incorporate these directives in his or her life. There's no need for a discipler to be a great Bible teacher; rather, he or she should be able to discern how to help others know which areas of their lives need change.

Both spiritually mature and strong in character, disciplers must be committed to their own personal growth in order to help others grow. They're humble and teachable, actively rehearsing the eleven practices essential to following Christ. In the process of discipling another, a discipler won't only grow to care about the other person more than he or she expected but will also find he or she is personally being changed.

What are the characteristics that should be evident in the life of a discipler?

Because they've been walking with Christ for some time, disciplers will already be striving to practice many, if not all, of the eleven practices essential to following Him. Their lives exhibit growing moral consistency and strength of character as they work to resist the continual temptations of our culture. Wisdom and understanding characterize their choices and decision making, yet they remain humble and teachable, offering respect for the insight of others. They possess a deepening self-awareness and an understanding not only of their own gifts but also their personal areas of brokenness.

Disciplers also have genuine concern for others and hearts to build into others' lives. They likely are part of active, authentic communities and are comfortably submitted to the leadership of their church communities.

How do you choose whom to disciple?

When determining whom to disciple, we strongly encourage you to invite someone into a discipleship relationship with whom you already have an existing connection. When two individuals already know each other, it's easier for them to gain traction and accelerate the potential for growth and depth. You should also look for certain characteristics within the person, which are below.

How many people can you disciple?

The ideal expression of The Way of Discipleship is one person discipling another person. When The Way of Discipleship is carried out in this manner, we believe the average discipler can handle between one and three disciples. The number you can handle depends on your experience in this realm. If this is your first time leading a discipleship relationship, we suggest you start with only one person. A discipleship relationship requires intentionality and time, including at least monthly gatherings. It also requires an organic aspect that involves time, energy, and emotional space.

How does a discipler best include a disciple in his or her life?

This depends on the existing relationship and the personality of both people involved. Your relationship with your disciple may already be at a place where you're experiencing life together, or it may grow into this. If this happens, that's a wonderful outworking of the relationship. However, it isn't a requirement that you spend considerable personal time with your disciple (and potentially his or her family) outside of your intentional gatherings.

Keep in mind that your growing relationship will involve a certain level of phone calls, texts, and e-mails between meetings. The amount of time dedicated to this depends on the relationship you cultivate. Regardless, you'll need to create time, heart, and passion for your disciple. This is why we recommend a discipler should begin by discipling one person at a time, in order to allow enough room for you to be part of the disciple's life.

How does your gender impact whom you disciple?

Because of the nature of the conversations and personal depth of sharing that we hope will occur through this relationship, only individuals of the same gender are to be involved in a discipleship relationship (i.e., men should disciple other men; women should disciple other women). We want to make sure that discipleship relationships don't invite temptation or appear compromising to others.

The Disciple

 ## What does it mean to be a disciple?

A disciple is a person who possesses an urgent and strong desire to grow in faith. Because disciples follow, they're willing to be led by someone in the process of helping them become more like Christ. Disciples are humble, being prepared to trust others to redirect them in any areas of their lives preventing them from growth and change. They're eager and ready to allow the Spirit of God to make them new.

What are the characteristics to look for in the life of a disciple?

Disciples should be eager to grow in their faith. This should be exhibited by a sense of urgency. They also should evidence a humble willingness to make the time it takes to be discipled. In addition, potential disciples should be open to the Holy Spirit's work in them and be open to correction and redirection. They should be willing to listen well. Finally, potential disciples should be aware of and open to the responsibility to replicate this type of relationship down the road.

What are some indications a person may not be ready to be a disciple?

Some indications that a disciple may not be ready for discipleship are a significant conflict in one or more of the disciple's personal relationships, a pattern of addiction in his or her life, and/or current life circumstances requiring a substantial amount of time, which limits his or her capacity to participate in discipleship (i.e., recent divorce, new marriage, new baby, etc.).

The Discipler/Disciple Relationship

 What does it mean for someone to follow me as I follow Jesus?

It's a bold and courageous thing to ask someone to follow you as you follow Jesus. Some would even say it's audacious and presumptuous to have that kind of relationship with another believer—a relationship that places you in a position of spiritual influence or spiritual authority. It's important to remember from where spiritual influence and spiritual authority come.

Spiritual influence and authority come from Christ-like character that's born out of brokenness. They're the result of experiencing the circumstances and choices in life that make you acutely aware of your weakness and dependence upon the transforming work of God's Spirit in your life. That transformation and the ongoing changes you're experiencing are what "qualify" you or "authorize" you to initiate and take the lead in an intentional disciple-making relationship. You aren't inviting someone to follow you because you're perfect. Rather, you're challenging another person to follow your example of learning to follow Jesus. And you're offering your experience and your transformed presence to help him or her.

People need direction and accountability in their spiritual lives. A person with an authoritative position can't always give personal direction or provide accountability as effectively as someone with authoritative presence in a relationship. As a discipler, you can have that kind of relationship and, as a result, that kind of influence.

This type of spiritual authority is illustrated in the Bible. Jesus conferred authority on His disciples when He challenged them to go out on His behalf, claiming that the harvest is plentiful but the workers are few. In Matthew 28, He reminds them that because He's with them, they walk with His authority. You, too, walk with His authority, which comes from His presence in your life.

Inviting someone into this type of relationship is scary, but it's also sacred. The sense of accountability goes both ways. Having spiritual influence and authority in another person's life brings great responsibility. In no way should a discipler ever have a sense of superiority or dominance over a disciple. The direction and accountability you offer to those you disciple should always be characterized by love, gentleness, and grace—the qualities that exemplify the presence of Christ in you as you guide others to follow Him.

How much of your personal story should you share with your disciple?

As the discipler, it's important to be willing to be open, honest, and prepared to disclose on a personal level. However, a discipler should use discernment in sharing and remember to never allow self-disclosure to be the main focus of a conversation.

To determine if you should share something from your own life, ask the following:

1. Does this person need to know this right now?
2. Is my story the best way to convey what he or she needs to hear?
3. Am I sharing this story because it's been so much about them that I need it to be about me?
4. What do I gain in the discipleship relationship by sharing this story? What does my disciple gain?
5. Are there people in this story who might be put in an unfavorable light if I tell this story?

How to Begin

 ## The Invitation

When inviting someone to enter into a discipleship relationship, you're asking the discipler to follow you as you follow Christ. Those with experience in calling people into this type of intentional relationship say the conversation can often turn into a sacred moment marked by tears, a physical posture of interest, an intense response, and a deep awareness on the part of both people of what's being asked of them.

We recommend that invitations be issued in person so that you'll be able to hear and see one another's response. If occasionally meeting with the person isn't already a normal part of your relationship, you might briefly introduce the idea over the phone and ask if he or she would be willing to get together with you in person to talk about it more.

In order to lay the groundwork for this type of sacred conversation, here are a few elements you should include in your initial invitation (you can also use the Getting Started section to guide your discussion):

- Introduce The Way of Discipleship (what is it?).
- Explain why you're asking him or her to follow you. What did you see in this person that caused you to issue this invitation?
- Share what you'll do when you meet. Make sure this person understands that this particular type of relationship will be focused on helping him or her more fully live out the eleven practices essential to following Christ, as compared to a general mentoring relationship.
- Discuss clear expectations of both the discipler and disciple in the relationship. Make sure he or she understands the time commitment in terms of how often you'll meet (about every two or three weeks), how he or she will need to explore each practice personally (through assigned reading, serving opportunities, practicing

spiritual disciplines, etc.), and the timeframe you're looking at (potentially a three-year relationship).

- Explain that near the end of your discipleship relationship, you'll be asking the disciple to begin discipling someone else.
- Explain that while you're planning to keep your conversations confidential, if something should come up that you don't know how to respond to, you'll consult with a member of the pastoral staff at your church.
- Ask for a decision. If the disciple isn't able to commit right then, make a plan as to when you'll follow up to find out his or her decision.

 ## What if he or she says yes?

Some people will be ready to commit to this type of discipleship relationship during your initial conversation, while others will need time to process what you're asking of them. Regardless of the timing of the response, it's important to discuss the following when someone accepts your invitation:

Schedule your first meeting.

Some find it best to schedule only one or two meetings at a time. Others prefer planning farther out and setting a regular time to meet. We recommend you commit to meeting approximately every three weeks. At a minimum, you should be meeting at least once a month with your disciple. Most discipleship pairs meet for about an hour and a half.

Determine where you want to meet.

You'll need to determine the best location based on where you both live and the environment that best allows for you to engage in intentional conversations. Keep in mind that places where you feel comfortable discussing your life might not feel comfortable to your disciple. You don't need to meet at the same place each time either. Pick places conducive to the different types of conversations you're having. Here are a few ideas to consider:

- Outdoor space—local parks, go on a walk, play golf, etc.
- Church
- Coffee shop

- Restaurant—Make sure you pick a restaurant where you won't feel rushed to give up your table and where you don't feel like other people are listening in on your conversation.
- Personal residence

What if he or she says no?

It's always hard to be turned down when you invite someone into this type of relationship. Try not to take it personally. Remember that Jesus was often rejected when He asked people to follow Him. You're asking for a big commitment. Some won't be ready to accept, due either to where they are in their faith or to their limited availability. Being a Christ follower means walking a narrow path that not everyone chooses to take.

While a gentle nudging can be helpful, make sure you don't push anyone to begin this relationship. Remember that Jesus *invited*—He never forced people to follow Him. If you sow a relationship with force, you'll sooner or later reap resentment.

If you're already in relationship with the person who declines your invitation, don't allow his or her decision to change your existing relationship. Pray for him or her and keep your sensors up for when he or she might be ready. Make sure the person understands that when ready, he or she should feel free to approach you to talk further.

If you find you're being turned down regularly by potential disciples, evaluate your approach. Think about who you're asking. What's the nature of your relationship with them? Remember that discipleship relationships work best when you already have an existing relationship with the person. Also, examine what you're asking them to do. Maybe they don't understand and you need to clarify your invitation. You might ask a trusted, mature friend what he or she sees in you that might be a barrier to people desiring to be discipled by you. Often we need others to help us see what we're unaware of. If you don't find that this helps, it might be appropriate for you to move into a discipleship relationship as a disciple. This will give you a chance to learn what this relationship can look like by watching someone else in this role.

Preparing for each meeting

Each discipler plans meetings differently. Some prefer to plan out six months to a year at a time; others prepare for only a few meetings down the road. Whatever method works best for you, make sure your time is directed toward the goal of your relationship—to intentionally explore together the eleven practices essential to following Christ. For "big picture" thinkers, a two-to-three-year relationship means you have approximately two months to spend on each practice in order to cover introductory topics and all eleven practices.

Preparing personally for each individual meeting is extremely important. This involves *regularly praying for your disciple* as you take responsibility for nurturing him or her spiritually. It also requires *spending quality time both examining the Scriptures and in introspective prayer* as you consider what the practice looks like in your own life. This enables you to continue to be shaped in your own understanding of the practice and to be transparent about your own struggle with incorporating each practice in your life.

Ongoing Meetings

 What does a typical meeting look like?

Relational connection

Start by briefly catching up on life. This communicates that you truly care about your disciple. Make sure you share from your own life as well. Questions you might ask include:

- How has your week been?
- What's going on in your life? Where have you seen God working in your life?
- How's work? Your family?
- You told me about *x* last time. Give me an update.
- What challenges have you been facing?

Accountability

Review what you talked about the last time you met and discuss how the disciple's understanding of that practice is developing. While the Guidebook provides direction, here are some other questions to consider:

- What do you sense that God is prompting in you as it relates to each practice, what you've read, a particular experience you've gone through, a discipline you've been practicing, etc.?
- What have you learned in the past few weeks?
- What has challenged you or is holding you back?
- What types of things are you thinking about right now or what questions are you asking?
- Are you noticing any patterns of God moving in your life right now?
- How are you feeling emotionally toward this topic? Why do you think you feel that way?

Determining next steps

Each time you meet, agree on a practical action step prior to your next gathering. Again, the Guidebook provides direction. Remember to challenge the disciple with things that will touch his or her heart and spirit and not just his or her mind. Make sure you vary the "next step" assignments. During your meeting, tell your disciple that you'll contact him or her later that week about what you want him or her to explore on his or her own before you get together again.

Ideas include:

- Look at a particular practice by reading the description in the discipleship manual and writing down three questions that come to mind. Have the disciple think through people in his or her life who are living out this practice and then come to the next meeting ready to share why he or she thinks those people are good examples.
- Read a particular passage of Scripture. Give your disciple a particular idea to think about as he or she is reading. You might challenge the disciple to read through the passage every other day or in different translations.
- Focus on one of the specific practices listed. As you get to know your disciple, the specific practices that might be more meaningful to him or her will become clear. Remember that the practices are only necessary as they help us live out what it means to be a disciple—they aren't the end goal.
- Choose a resource or two from the online resources page at thewayofdiscipleship.org to read or participate in together.
- Consider a list of reflection questions you've provided the disciple.

Closing

Although you might not choose to pray at the end of every meeting, establishing it as a common practice of your time together will deepen your relationship and enhance your time. You may wish to take the lead on your closing prayer at your first few meetings; however, it'll be helpful to ask the disciple to begin to pray after your intentional relationship has gotten underway.

Ideas for concluding the meeting in prayer include:

- beginning by referencing the disciple's personal life, mentioning any issues he or she may have shared during your meeting;
- lifting up any concerns the disciple shared; and
- closing by asking the Lord for His guidance, wisdom, and power as the disciple continues to move forward in making the eleven practices part of his or her daily life.

Summarizing

As a discipler, make sure you mentally or physically record things you want to explore further in future meetings. Some people find it helpful to jot down thoughts or questions in a notebook immediately after meeting with their disciples, reviewing it prior to their next meetings. And remember, the more we encourage disciples to initiate and own their spiritual growth, the better. The goal is for disciples to develop their own spiritual growth for their lifetimes.

Follow up

Three to four days prior to your next meeting, send an e-mail reminder to your disciple recapping what you asked him or her to do when you last met. Remind the disciple that if he or she isn't prepared for your next meeting, to please let you know so you can reschedule for a later date when the disciple has had a chance to prepare for the meeting.

How do you know when to move to the next practice?

The practices aren't meant to be perfected. Each is a life-long, ongoing practice. Even though the guidebook recommends three to four sessions per practice, there's no need to rush. Once you're comfortable that your disciple understands the practice and its importance in his or her life and you believe your disciple is familiar with several of the disciplines related to the practice, you can consider moving to the next practice. The best indicator will be practical changes you notice in your disciple's life that you can affirm.

Multiplication

In order to help a person get ready to begin his or her own discipleship relationship, strategically focus on the Practice of *Leading Others to Jesus*. This practice serves as a great launching pad into the conversation regarding beginning a discipleship relationship. Talk about how this practice isn't just about leading people to Christ for the first time but also about one's development as a follower of Christ. Make sure the disciple understands that his or her present relationship with you is part of this larger practice.

To help someone prepare for the role of a discipler, you might consider switching roles while studying the final two practices, having your disciple walk *you* through each practice. This will provide the disciple a valuable training experience where you can offer feedback.

Signs that a disciple is ready to take this lead role:

- Obvious signs of personal growth and transformation that come from the integration of the eleven practices into daily life. The disciple doesn't need to be an expert, but he or she must have seriously studied the practices and be actively attempting to integrate them into his or her life.
- A good understanding of the Practice of Leading Others to Jesus.
- Approaching his or her existing discipleship relationship with a level of seriousness, engagement, and commitment that shows the disciple is ready to move forward.
- Having a context for relationships where the disciple can invite someone to begin to follow him or her. You shouldn't have to coax the disciple to go find someone to disciple.

Closure

Ongoing Relationship between Disciple and Discipler

Once you've completed your formal discipleship relationship, you might wonder what your involvement in the disciple's life will continue to be. We suggest you have some kind of follow-up plan. This won't only support your disciple as he or she moves into leading his or her own discipleship relationship, but it'll also provide accountability to the disciple as he or she continues to live out the eleven practices on a personal level. This follow-up plan might be checking in monthly or quarterly for the first year after the formal relationship ends. You'll also want to make sure the disciple knows the door is always open for him or her to approach you for further coaching and support.

After this point, because of the amount of time you spent together, it's nearly impossible to walk away completely from your relationship (nor do we recommend that). Most disciplers find that the relationship turns into a lifelong coaching relationship. Others discover that theirs has evolved into a deep, spiritual friendship where they begin to function as co-disciples, mutually supporting each other.

Listening Skills

Ten Ways to Be a Better Listener

1. **Be quiet.** This should be obvious but it often is the biggest obstruction to listening. The leader should be part of a discussion without monopolizing it.
2. **Try to understand.** The goal of listening is to understand what the person is really saying.
3. **Eliminate distractions.** People feel comfortable sharing when they aren't interrupted. Turn the phone ringer off. Make sure you have childcare arranged. Don't look at your watch or lesson plan when someone is speaking.
4. **Empathize.** Interject short statements to show you understand and accept what the person is saying. "That sounds exciting!" or, "That must've been a hard decision to make," are good examples of how to show empathy.
5. **Don't judge.** Especially when someone is already hurting, a judgmental attitude can do more harm than good. Don't condone sin, of course, but recognize the difference between acceptance and approval.
6. **Avoid advising.** Unless they ask for it, people usually don't want or need you to try to solve their problems. They just need someone to listen.
7. **Verify and clarify.** If you don't understand what someone's saying, ask: "Here's what I hear you saying: '_____.' Am I right?" is one good clarifier.
8. **Listen for what isn't said.** Try to hear the meaning behind the words. Watch body language and listen to tone of voice. Sometimes what a person is saying is lost behind a clutter of words. A person's posture or gestures can say more than words.
9. **Affirm.** "Thanks for sharing that. I'm sure it isn't easy to talk about it right now." This builds acceptance for talking about difficult things and makes it easier for someone else to share.

Adapted from materials by Mike Mack, cofounder of Smallgroups.com. www.churchleaders. com/smallgroups/small-group-how-tos/145093-10-ways-to-be-a-better-listener.html

Asking Open-Ended Questions

Overview

Closed-ended questions can be answered with single one or two-word responses. They are often yes or no questions and don't leave much room for elaboration, interpretation, or opinion.

Open-ended questions, on the other hand, are questions that can't be answered with one-word responses. They require some thought and some details to reasonably answer.

Build a conversation.

Simple, closed-ended questions don't leave much room for elaboration or really a full response. These are often questions using phrases like *did you, when, do you want to, will you, have you,* etc. Each of these just needs a couple words to answer, and they don't transition well from one topic to another in a conversation. They leave little room for new ideas, and they don't spark much creativity or imagination or lead to new questions.

That's where open-ended questions excel. They provide much more detail, thoughts, comments, and bits of information that can more easily form into new ideas and transitions. Here are some examples of typical questions in an open format:

- Tell me what you think about that.
- What is it you like about the idea?
- Why would you suggest that?
- How do you plan to achieve that?

Let others talk more than you

Open-ended questions also ensure that you give others a chance to talk more than you. It forces you to listen more in any conversation because you have to wait for a longer response with these questions. You can still lead a conversation by steering with your questions, but the open-ended questions will allow room for a more elaborate response.

Open-ended questioning is also a great tool to promote creative thought, problem-solving skills, and cognitive growth in others because it forces them to spend more time contemplating their response instead of just giving a disconnected yes or no response.

Ask them to talk about themselves.

Similarly to simply having someone talk more, having someone talk about him- or herself and his or her own thoughts and feelings on a subject shows that you have some genuine interest in that person and care enough to want to take the time to listen. This is immensely powerful both for seeing how the conversation topics affect that person and for strengthening that relationship more. Whether you know the person well or are already a close friend or family member, these personal and open-ended questions lead to an even stronger bond with a longer, more meaningful conversation at the onset.

Examples of open-ended questions:

- What does that mean to you?
- How did you go about solving that problem?
- What prompted you to make that choice?
- What information do you have about that?
- What would you do differently next time?
- What does that feeling come from?

All information (except example questions) came from "Open Ended Questions Make Better Conversations," *Learn This*, last modified December 2, 2008, *http://learnthis.ca/2008/12/open-ended-questions-make-better-conversations*.

Example questions came from "Examples of Open-Ended Questions" accessed August 28, 2014, *http://wiki.answers.com/Q/What_are_20_examples_of_open_ended_questions*.

Barriers to Growth

The following scenarios represent situations that could occur to you as a discipler. For further advice, we encourage you to contact a member of the pastoral staff at your church.

Scenario 1: Lack of Commitment

The person I'm discipling shows a lack of commitment. He or she doesn't show up and often doesn't do the assignment. He or she says the relationship is important, but his or her actions don't seem to support that.

Start by having a loving, honest conversation about what you're seeing. It's better to communicate what you're seeing upfront instead of holding things in. Ask if you're reading your disciple's actions—or lack of actions—wrong by saying, "I'm observing you doing this: _____. Am I wrong? If I'm wrong, help me understand why. What am I not seeing correctly?"

Make sure that through this conversation you get to the bottom of the issue. It's OK to lovingly agree that it's not the right time or the right match for the discipler-disciple relationship. If he or she needs a break, share that you'll be calling in a month or two to see how things are and to see if he or she is ready to pick up meeting again. If he or she is lacking a connection with you and wants to switch disciplers, see if you're able to connect him or her with someone else.

If after several conversations you still don't see change, warn him or her that if nothing changes, you won't be able to continue meeting. If he or she is unwilling to comply, you need to stop discipling the person, because it's not worth the investment of time in someone who isn't actively engaging in the process.

Scenario 2: Avoidance and Lack of Openness

The person I'm discipling is reticent to disclose his or her life with me or is avoiding me.

Oftentimes, people begin avoiding others or stop sharing because they feel trapped and judged by the incongruence between what you're exploring through the eleven practices and their own lives. When this happens, start by acknowledging that the process can bring up these incongruences. If appropriate, acknowledge that you have had a similar experience. This affirms that the process of our brokenness surfacing is normal and necessary for the healing we all need. Often this will be all the disciple needs to move forward. Look for and celebrate the small steps the disciple takes and how they often lead to great change.

Scenario 3: Lack of Life Change

What do you do when your disciple isn't making any changes to his or her lifestyle?

Have an honest conversation about what you're seeing. To do this, ask if you're reading his or her actions—or lack of actions—wrong by saying, "I'm not observing you making the lifestyle changes we've been talking about when we meet. Am I wrong? If I'm wrong, help me understand why. What am I not seeing correctly? What do you think is holding you back?" Don't assume or jump to conclusions; seek to understand.

Listen carefully to see whether he or she truly isn't open to life change, or if he or she is open but struggling to actually make the necessary changes. As you listen, you might find there are other life situations present you're unaware of that are making it hard for him or her to truly make changes. As things come to the surface, remind yourself that your job isn't to fix your disciple but instead to offer God's healing through your presence. As situations come to light, refer him or her to resources that might be helpful. A list of recommended resources for various life situations is available at thewayofdiscipleship.org.

If after several conversations your disciple is unwilling to take steps toward change, you may choose to stop meeting with him or her until he or she takes action. Discipleship is about our lives becoming more like Christ's. Some people will ultimately choose not to follow that path.

Scenario 4: Morality Issues

How do I deal with unexpected morality issues that come up?

In the midst of an intentional relationship like this, it's common to find out things that are very personal and sometimes have been held as secrets for years. Don't be surprised by anything you hear. Remember that it's not your responsibility to fix whatever's wrong or be an expert on getting the person out of the situation. Instead, your presence is often part of God's way of bringing healing to your disciple, and the safety of your presence is what he or she needs most. Whether you realize it or not, your presence goes a long way in someone's healing by allowing him or her to feel and experience the graciousness of God through you as a discipler. Oftentimes the biggest problem is the secrecy. Once a person has expressed a secret, it often becomes easier to be honest about everything in his or her life.

If an issue comes up that causes you to be uncertain about how to proceed, seek counsel from a trusted discipler or a member of the pastoral staff at your church. In order to gain further trust with your disciple, tell him or her ahead of time you're going to seek further counsel. If an issue comes up that's significantly immoral or dangerous, seek counsel from the pastoral staff at your church.

When to Get Outside Help

During the discipleship relationship, it's possible that you'll uncover hidden issues resulting from difficult life circumstances or brokenness. The discipler and disciple will both need courage to address these hidden issues in the disciple's life. You also may need additional resources and help.

Flags indicating a disciple might need additional help

- He or she begins avoiding you. This might be because the practices are bringing to life the incongruence between what you're talking about and his or her life.
- He or she becomes argumentative, continually confronting and challenging you.
- He or she mentions his or her spouse is resistant to changes beginning to result from the discipleship relationship.
- He or she isn't able to carry out the functions of daily living.
- Depression or anxiety inhibits him or her from engaging.
- He or she shows severe inconsistency in his or her life.
- He or she alludes to any type of addictive brokenness. This is when he or she uses a normal substance, behavior, or relationship(s) in a progressively abnormal way that eventually masters him or her.
- You hear him or her repetitively bringing up a pattern of a problem.
- He or she continually refers to significant challenges in his or her life, including marital, financial, parenting, etc.
- He or she seems to be stuck in past hurts or patterns and isn't able to move forward.

Inductive Bible Study

Inductive Bible study is a method that involves three skills: observation, interpretation, and application.

Observation: Discover what it says.

1. **Ask the "Five Ws and an H."**

    As you study any passage of Scripture, train yourself to constantly ask: **Who? What? When? Where? Why? How?** These questions are the building blocks of precise **observation**, which is essential for accurate **interpretation**.

2. **Mark key words and phrases.**

    A key word is one that's essential to the text. Key words and phrases are often repeated in order to convey the author's point or purpose for writing. It's also helpful to mark key words using symbols, colors, or a combination of the two.

3. **Make lists.**

    Making lists can be one of the most enlightening things you do as you study. Lists reveal truths and highlight important concepts. It can be helpful to make a list of what you learn about each key word you mark.

4. **Watch for contrasts and comparisons.**

    Contrasts and comparisons use highly descriptive language to make it easier to remember what you've learned. For example, in 1 Peter 5:8, Peter compares the devil to a roaring lion. In the same letter, Peter contrasts God's attitude toward the proud and the humble.

5. **Note expressions of time.**

   The relationship of events in time often sheds light on the true meaning of the text. Marking them will help you see the sequence or timing of events and lead to accurate interpretation of Scripture.

6. **Pay attention to geographic locations.**

   Often it's helpful to mark geographical locations that show you where an event takes place.

7. **Mark terms of conclusion.**

   Words such as "therefore," "thus," and "for this reason" indicate that a conclusion or summary is being made. You may want to underline them in the text.

8. **Identify chapter themes.**

   The theme or "big idea" of a chapter will center on the main person, event, teaching, or subject of that section of Scripture. Themes are often revealed by reviewing the key words and lists you developed. Try to express the theme as briefly as possible, using words found in the text.

Interpretation—Discover what it means.

While **observation** leads to an accurate understanding of what the Word of God *says*, **interpretation** goes a step further and helps you understand what it *means*. As you seek to interpret the Bible accurately, the following guidelines will be helpful:

1. **Remember that context rules.**

   If you lay the solid foundation of observation, you'll be prepared to consider each verse in the light of the surrounding verses, the book in which it's found, and the entire Word of God. As you study, ask yourself: Is my interpretation of a passage of Scripture consistent with the theme, purpose, and structure of the book in which it's found? Is it consistent with other Scripture about the same subject? Am I considering the historic and cultural context? Never take a Scripture out of its context to make it say what you want it to say. Discover what the author is saying; don't add to his meaning.

2. Always seek the full counsel of the Word of God.

When you know God's Word thoroughly, you won't accept a teaching simply because someone has used one or two isolated verses to support it. You'll be able to discern whether a teaching is biblical or not. Saturate yourself in the Word of God; it's your safeguard against wrong doctrine.

3. Don't base your convictions on an obscure passage of Scripture.

An obscure passage is one in which the meaning isn't easily understood. Because these passages are difficult to understand even when proper principles of interpretation are used, they shouldn't be used as bases for establishing doctrine.

4. Interpret Scripture carefully.

God spoke to us that we might know truth about Him. Therefore, take the Word of God at face value—in its natural, normal sense. Look first for the clear teaching of Scriptures, not a hidden meaning. Understand and recognize figures of speech and interpret them accordingly.

Consider what's being said in the light of its literary style. For example, you'll find more similes and metaphors in poetical and prophetic literature than in historical or biographical books. Interpret portions of Scripture according to their literary styles.

Some literary styles in the Bible are
- historical—Acts,
- prophetic—Revelation,
- biographical—Luke,
- didactic (teaching)—Romans,
- poetic—Psalms,
- epistle (letter)—2 Timothy, and
- proverbial—Proverbs.

5. Look for the single meaning of the passage.

Always try to understand what the author had in mind when you interpret a portion of the Bible. Don't twist verses to support a meaning that isn't clearly taught. Unless the author of a particular book indicates that there's another meaning to what he says, let the passage speak for itself.

Application—Discover How it Works

The first step in application is to find out what the Word of God says on any particular subject through accurate observation and correct interpretation of the text. Paul said that all Scripture is inspired by God and profitable for teaching, for reproof, for correction, for training in righteousness; so that the man of God may be adequate, equipped for every good work (2 Timothy 3:16–17). A correct interpretation will often lead to reproof, correction, or encouragement.

Reproof exposes areas of your thinking and behaving that don't align with God's Word. Reproof is finding out where you've thought wrongly or haven't been doing what God says is right. The application of reproof is to accept it and agree with God, acknowledging where you are wrong in thought or in behavior.

Correction is the next step in application and often the most difficult. Many times correction comes by simply confessing and forsaking what's wrong. Other times, God gives very definite steps for you to take.

Encouragement is the application that confirms that you belong to God and that His desire is to bring His kingdom into His world through you.

This inductive Bible study overview is adapted from Precept Ministries International. http://precept.org/data/sites/1/PDFs/PMI_IBStudyOverview_v2.pdf

Spiritual Disciplines

In order to incorporate the overall eleven practices into our lives, each practice uses a handful of the following specific spiritual disciplines, like tools in a toolbox used for particular purposes. The following is a glossary of those disciplines in alphabetical order.

abstinence	Abstinence is a longer form of fasting through avoidance of any specific thing, such as alcoholic beverages, meat, or sexual activity, with the intent of focusing on a godly life.
accountability	Accountability is resolving to engage in relationships with others for the purpose of providing an honest perspective and rebuke, when necessary.
asceticism	Asceticism is a more extreme form of simplicity characterized by a sacrificial lifestyle.
baptism	Baptism is a public statement and ceremony of commitment and surrender to Christ, symbolizing the death of the old life and the beginning of a new life.
breath prayers	Breath prayers are short prayers we utter frequently to refocus us on the constant presence of God.
communion	Communion (the Lord's Supper, Eucharist) is a sacrament or ceremony of remembering the death and resurrection of Jesus through eating and drinking of the symbols of the bread and the cup.
confession	Confession is an honest admission to God of ways you've sinned and desire to repent.
contemplative prayer	Contemplative prayer is prayer without words to cultivate attentiveness and listening to God.

corporate prayer	Corporate prayer is engaging with others in conversation with God about what He and we are thinking, feeling, and doing together.
corporate worship	Corporate worship expresses through words, art, music, rituals, and silent adoration the greatness, beauty, and goodness of God.
debt elimination	Debt elimination is the deliberate process of paying off loans and committing to live without borrowing, so as to be free from financial worry and free to contribute generously to God's work.
devotional Bible reading	Devotional Bible reading (*Lectio Divina*, Latin for sacred reading) is the repetitive, thoughtful reading and contemplation of Scripture passages with an attitude of surrender and openness.
fasting	Fasting is temporarily abstaining from eating food, electronic media, television, etc. for a period of time with the purpose of focusing on prayer and spiritual guidance.
fellowship	Fellowship is engaging with other disciples in the common activities of worship, study, prayer, celebration, and service that sustain our lives together and enlarge our capacity to experience more of God.
hospitality	Hospitality is inviting others into our homes and lives to build relationships for natural opportunities to share our faith.
inductive Bible study	Inductive Bible study involves reading a book of the Bible and studying the history and context of the story while also determining how that story might apply to us today.
intentional friendship	Intentional friendship is the practice of engaging in natural relationships with those in our lives (work, neighborhood, community, and family) so as to have the opportunity to lead them to Jesus.
intercessory prayer	Intercessory prayer is spending time praying directly for the people around us who are far from Jesus, asking God to reveal ways we can engage them in the conversation.
investigating your spiritual gifts	Investigating your spiritual gifts is the process of learning your unique spiritual gift mix to help you discover what God is calling you to do in service to him and others.
journaling	Journaling consists of keeping a personal record of your life experiences, faith journey, and reflections of the Bible.

meditative prayer	Meditative prayer is focused concentration and reflection on something God has said through Scripture.
memorization	Memorization is a careful, repetitive meditation on certain passages of Scripture so as to set them to memory and have them available to recall at any time as you respond to life circumstances.
peacemaking	Peacemaking is the process of encouraging constructive resolution of conflict between individuals, people groups, races, or countries.
personal budgeting	Personal budgeting consists of establishing a planned level of expenditures at a detailed level and sticking to it.
purposeful community	Purposeful community is intentionally sharing life with a small group of people for study, prayer, care, and accountability.
Sabbath	Sabbath is a specific period of rest from the labors of life for the purpose of rejuvenation and fellowship with God and one another.
self-examination	Self-examination is the process of reflecting deeply on the state of one's soul, particularly one's conduct, motives, and desires.
serving others	Serving others is using one's unique passions, abilities, and spiritual gifts as a way to love God and love others.
serving the poor and marginalized	Serving the poor and marginalized is the process of releasing one's own agenda and need for accomplishment and humbly submitting oneself to be in the presence of the poor and marginalized.
silence	Silence is the discipline of unplugging from noise and words, stilling the mind and heart, and practicing the presence of being with God.
simplicity	Simplicity is the choice to scale down the consumption and busyness of life, living purposely with less and choosing to do less.
solitude	Solitude is the discipline of being alone, freeing oneself from the distraction of people as to give oneself completely to God.
studying the Bible and apologetics	Studying the Bible and apologetics involves taking time to understand what we believe and why, so as to be able to convey this to others.
studying the word of God in community	Studying the Word of God in community is discussing the Bible and learning with others in a small group.

submitting to a mentor	Submitting to a mentor is the process of meeting with a trusted individual for particular guidance in an area of your spiritual life.
tithing/giving	Tithing is the setting aside of at least 10 percent of your gross income to be given to your church and other kingdom-serving organizations.
vow of faithfulness or chastity	A vow of faithfulness is the commitment to stay true to your marriage vows with fidelity and devotion, while a vow of chastity is the commitment to refrain from sex outside the covenant of marriage.

Grace Church Statement of Belief

What we believe at Grace Church:

God: We believe there's only one true God who is eternal, all-powerful, all-knowing, just and loving. We believe God purposefully created the world and is personally engaged in the lives of human beings.

Humanity: We believe every person is uniquely created in the image of God but, through sinful disobedience, is broken and has alienated him- or herself from God, others, and the creation. The result is that every person is in need of healing and reconciliation.

Jesus Christ: We believe God entered the world in human form in the person of Jesus Christ; Jesus Christ is both fully human and completely God. Jesus alone reconciled us with God, revealed God's character, and inaugurated God's kingdom.

Kingdom: We believe God's kingdom is the sum of His purposes and hopes for this world. The kingdom is realized as Christ's disciples commit themselves to His mission. We anticipate a future time when Jesus will return to complete the mission of God on earth.

Salvation: We believe that, through faith in Jesus' life, death and resurrection, our sinful disobedience is forgiven and that, through repentance and surrender to God, we're reconciled to Him for this life and eternity.

Holy Spirit: We believe the Holy Spirit is God's indwelling presence: the source of power, guidance and conviction in the life of a follower of Christ.

Church: We believe the Church is the universal community of all Christ followers. The Church finds its best expression in unique, local communities of Christ followers united for the purpose of evidencing the values of the kingdom of God in the world.

Bible: We believe the Bible was written by human authors under the supernatural inspiration of God and is our authority for all matters of faith and practice.

Planning Calendar

Agree on a common place: _____, day: _____, and time: _____. (60–90 minutes). Plug these dates into smartphones or your home calendar. Schedule sessions about every two weeks. If there's a conflict, reschedule right away, even if you have to do it over the phone, Skype, or FaceTime. Evaluate your rhythm often.

Practice	Sessions	Dates	Notes
Getting Started	3	1. 2. 3.	
Practices That Deepen your Roots			
Surrender and Trust	3	1. 2. 3.	
Communion with God	3	1. 2. 3.	
Studying the Word of God	3	1. 2. 3.	
Practices That Provide Stability			
Self-Denial	3	1. 2. 3	

Moral Integrity	3	1. 2. 3.	
Spiritual Community	3	1. 2. 3.	
Practices That Branch Out and Bear Fruit			
Seeking the Call of God	4	1. 2. 3. 4.	
Justice and Mercy	3	1. 2. 3.	
Material Generosity	3	1. 2. 3.	
Loving Others Well	3	1. 2. 3.	
Leading Others to Jesus	3	1. 2. 3.	
Passing the Baton	3	1. 2. 3.	
	40		

References

Ahlberg Calhoun, A. *Spiritual Disciplines Handbook: Practices That Transform Us*. Downers Grove: InterVarsity Press, 2005.

Allender, D. *Bold Love*. Colorado Springs: NavPress, 1992.

Barton, R. H. *Sacred Rhythms: Arranging Our Lives for Spiritual Transformation*. Downers Grove: InterVarsity Press, 2006.

———. *Strengthening the Soul of Your Leadership: Seeking God in the Crucible of Ministry*. Downers Grove: InterVarsity Press, 2008.

———. *Invitation to Solitude and Silence: Experiencing God's Transforming Presence*. Downers Grove: InterVarsity Press, 2010.

Bonhoeffer, D. *The Cost of Discipleship*. New York: Touchstone, 1995.

Buchanan, M. *Your God Is Too Safe: Rediscovering the Wonder of a God You Can't Control*. Grand Rapids: Multnomah, 2001.

———. *The Rest of God: Restoring Your Soul by Restoring Sabbath*. Nashville: Thomas Nelson, 2006.

Buechner, F. *Wishful Thinking: A Seeker's ABC*. New York: Harper One, 1993.

Burkett, L. *The Word on Finances*. Chicago: Moody Press, 1994.

Caliguire, M. *Soul Searching*. Downers Grove: InterVarsity Press, 2008.

Cloud, H. *Integrity*. New York: HarperCollins, 2006.

Guinness, O. *The Call: Finding and Fulfilling the Central Purpose of Your Life*. Nashville: Thomas Nelson, 2003.

Hatmaker, J. *7: An Experimental Mutiny Against Excess*. Nashville: B&H, 2012.

Henderson, J. *Evangelism Without Additives: What if sharing your faith meant just being yourself?* Colorado Springs: WaterBrook Press, 2007.

Hybels, B. *Who You Are When No One's Looking: Choosing Consistency, Resisting Compromise*. Downers Grove: InterVarsity Press, 1987.

———. *Just Walk Across the Room: Simple Steps Pointing People to Faith*. Grand Rapids: Zondervan, 2006.

Lewis, C. S. *Mere Christianity*. New York: HarperCollins, 2006.

Manning, B. *Ruthless Trust: The Ragamuffin's Path to God.* New York: HarperCollins, 2000.

Ogden, G. *Transforming Discipleship: Making Disciples a Few at a Time.* Downers Grove: InterVarsity Press, 2003.

Ortberg, J. *The Life You've Always Wanted.* Grand Rapids: Zondervan, 1998.

———. *The Me I Want to Be: Becoming God's Best Version of You.* Grand Rapids: Zondervan, 2009.

———. *Who Is This Man?: The Unpredictable Impact of the Inescapable Jesus.* Grand Rapids: Zondervan, 2012.

Samson, W., and L. Samson. *Justice in the Burbs: Being the Hands of Jesus Wherever You Live.* Grand Rapids: Baker Books, 2007.

Sider, R. *Just Generosity: A New Vision for Overcoming Poverty in America.* Grand Rapids: Baker Books, 2007.

Smith, C. *Soul Searching: The Religious and Spiritual Lives of American Teenagers.* New York: Oxford University Press, 2005.

Smith, J. B. *The Good and Beautiful Community: Following the Spirit, Extending Grace, Demonstrating Love.* Downers Grove: InterVarsity Press, 2010.

Stearns, R. *The Hole in Our Gospel: What Does God Expect of Us? The Answer That Changed My Life and Might Just Change the World.* Nashville: Thomas Nelson, 2010.

Tozer, A. W. *The Pursuit of God.* Ventura: Gospel Light, 2013.

Yancey, P. *Prayer: Does It Make Any Difference?* Grand Rapids: Zondervan, 2010.

About the editor: Ron Stohler serves as a Pastor of Adult Ministries at Grace Church in Central Indiana and is driven by a passion to help people find their true identity in Christ and calling in this world. He has served on staff with Grace for 17 years, 10 years with DuPont in marketing communications, holds a MAGL from Fuller Theological Seminary and BA from the University of Delaware. He married his college sweetheart and has three grown children.

GRACE
CHURCH

Made in the USA
Middletown, DE
27 May 2015